D1203364

All 45 Commanders in Chief

AMERICA'S PRESIDENTS

RANKED FROM BEST TO WORST

CENTENNIAL BOOKS

OATH OF OFFICE

"I do solemnly swear that I will faithfully execute the Office of President of the United States, and will to the best of my ability, preserve, protect and defend the Constitution of the United States."

CONTENTS

★ ★ ★

6

22

180

WHAT IS THE
PRESIDENCY?

THIS MAY COME AS A SURPRISE, BUT THE PRESIDENT OF THE UNITED STATES OF AMERICA IS NOT THE HIGHEST OFFICER IN THE LAND— YOU ARE

★ ★

DID YOU KNOW?

Among the perks for former presidents is a staff paid for by taxpayers and free postage for life.

THE CITIZEN IS THE HIGHEST-RANKED INDIVIDUAL IN America. The U.S. Constitution was explicit in that, and as President Franklin D. Roosevelt said, "Presidents are selected, not elected."

The president of the United States is the head of the executive branch—but has, unfortunately, come to be viewed by some as a kind of supreme leader, with all the trappings of an emperor. It's a complete misperception: He or she is a public servant (and accepts that very role when taking the oath of office) who works for you, despite William Howard Taft's venting, "It seems to be the profession of a president simply to hear other people talk."

Thomas Jefferson may have summed up the presidency best, writing, "No man will ever bring out of that office the reputation which carries him into it. The honeymoon would be as short in that case as in any other, and its moments of ecstasy would be ransomed by years of torment and hatred."

Originally, Congress assumed more authority than the president, but over the past 200-plus years the man (and so far, it has only been a man) in the role has increased the influence and power of the position. The presidents with the strongest personalities (and, in the best cases, vision) dictated and pushed through more of the policies they wanted and guided the country's will more by force of charisma than the rights of the office.

Maybe that's because being president is not easy, as Gene Healy wrote in *The Cult of the Presidency: America's Dangerous Devotion to Executive Power.* "Americans expect the president to right the wrongs that plague us—and we blame him when he fails. Because we invest impossible expectations in the presidency, the presidency has become an impossible job. And once the honeymoon period inevitably fades, the modern president becomes a lightning rod for discontent, often catching blame for phenomena beyond the control of any one person, however powerful."

But a president needs to unite America, especially during contentious times. A president needs to give the people hope for a prosperous future for themselves and their families. The policies proposed, imposed and vetoed are meant to be in the best interest of the country, putting personal, religious and political feelings aside.

The requirements to become president are simple enough: The person, man or woman, has to be 35 years old—although in 1787, and for almost another 150 years, women didn't even have the right to vote, so the thought of one becoming president was not top of mind—and a natural-born American citizen who has lived in the U.S. for at least 14 years.

A president can now serve only two terms, something the first one, George Washington, more or less suggested when he chose not to run for a third term, believing that for a democracy to be strong, there should be no sense of the presidency being an appointment for life, and that new leadership should constantly be brought in. It actually didn't become a law until after Franklin D. Roosevelt died in office in the early months of his fourth term.

The president, contrary to common perception, cannot declare war—only Congress can. As commander in chief, the president can authorize military action in national emergencies but is mandated to get Congress' approval for any action beyond 100 days. The president is also the only person who can order the use of nuclear weapons. In addition to running the Executive Branch, the president is considered the chief diplomat of the U.S. and responsible for the direction of foreign policy.

This country was formed to reject a monarchy, not recast one, although over time, through subtle erosion by politics and a public's exponential indifference, the distinction has been substantially worn away. Today, we refer to the president as the most powerful person in the world, and as commander in chief the president could at any moment certainly be the most dangerous person, since he has the world's most vast and destructive arsenal at his fingertips. But that's not the same thing. Yet whoever is president greatly matters. His (or her) actions, seen and heard around the world, are a reflection of our nation and us: we the people.

—*Bob Guccione, Jr.*

★ ★ ★

BIRTH
— of a —
NATION

AMERICA'S FOUNDING FATHERS WERE
REVOLUTIONARY. BUT WHO WERE THEY?

★ ★ ★

"FOUR SCORE AND SEVEN YEARS AGO OUR FATHERS BROUGHT forth, upon this continent, a new nation, conceived in liberty, and dedicated to the proposition that all men are created equal." Abraham Lincoln's Gettysburg Address in 1863 famously sums up the accomplishments of the founders of the United States. But who were they, exactly?

Certainly, some of the names are still well known, including George Washington, Alexander Hamilton, Thomas Jefferson and Benjamin Franklin. But the "fathers," who would later become known as the "Founding Fathers" when Warren G. Harding coined the phrase in his 1916 address to the Republican National Convention, were actually a group of revolutionaries who helped build a young nation through the Continental Congress that united 13 colonies, the signing of the Declaration of Independence and the Revolutionary War.

The time of the Founding Fathers, as described by Joseph Ellis in *American Creation: Triumphs and Tragedies in the Founding of the Republic*, was "the most politically creative era in American history."

The story of the Founding Fathers, and of the origin of the United States of America, begins in Philadelphia in 1774, at the First Continental Congress. There, members of the 12 of the 13 colonies (only Georgia, which relied on British military assistance to fight off a Native American uprising, was absent) met to discuss a response to Great Britain's punishment of Massachusetts, known as the Intolerable Acts, following the Tea Party rebellion over British tariffs. Parliament had stripped the colony of self-governance and started a blockade of Boston's port, leading to protests from the other colonies. Among the delegates to the First Continental Congress were many of the wealthy

The "Committee of Five" helped put together the Declaration of Independence.

The British surrendered at the Battle of Yorktown in 1781, ushering in the end of the Revolutionary War.

plantation owners, businessmen and attorneys who would come to be known as Founding Fathers, including Washington, "Father of the American Revolution" Samuel Adams, future U.S. president John Adams and the fiery orator Patrick Henry, who is most known for his famous declaration, "give me liberty or give me death," made during a speech at the Virginia Convention in 1775.

The First Continental Congress concluded after 51 days of debates and discussions, with delegates sending responses to Britain that ranged from aggressive to conciliatory. "The Declaration of Rights," for instance, pledged continued loyalty to Great Britain while rebelling against taxation. The British response, the Restraining Act of 1775, prevented New England colonies from trading with any partners except Great Britain, and banned fishing, shutting off a main food supply. Tensions escalated and skirmishes broke out in New England between the Patriots and the British forces, leading to the American Revolutionary War.

After the war was underway, the Second Continental Congress convened in Philadelphia in 1775, leading to many of the seminal events in U.S.

history. Here, the delegates created the Continental Army and named George Washington as its commander in chief. Even as this was happening, many residents in the colonies didn't espouse a break with Britain, but a pamphlet titled "Common Sense," written by British expatriate Thomas Paine and calling for a break from the Crown in plain terms, began to sway public opinion. Among its many well-known quotes, the document included the line "For all men being originally equals," which are thought to have influenced the Founding Fathers (and which lead some historians to claim that Paine was himself a Founding Father).

The Congress continued to meet, and by 1776, delegates from Virginia and other colonies began calling for independence from Great Britain. A group known as the "Committee of Five" brought together Franklin (from Pennsylvania), Adams (Massachusetts), Robert Livingston (New York), Roger Sherman (Connecticut) and Jefferson (Virginia), who was the main author of the document that helped shape America, the Declaration of Independence. Committee members Franklin and Adams made minor revisions to Jefferson's text and a few major ones—including removing a section blaming Britain's King George III for the transatlantic slave trade. On July 4, 1776, the Congress voted to approve the Declaration of Independence. Fifty-six men signed the document, including the president of Congress, John Hancock, whose fanciful signature led to his name becoming synonymous with signing important documents.

The Declaration of Independence's preamble, which Lincoln would reference 87 years later in his Gettysburg Address, remains its most enduring passage: "We hold these truths to be self-evident; that all men are created equal; that they are endowed by their Creator with certain inalienable rights; that among these are life, liberty and the pursuit of happiness; that to secure these rights, governments are instituted among men, deriving their just powers from the consent of the governed."

The decision to renounce British rule marked a major turning point and allowed the colonies to

The Declaration of Independence was signed by 56 men, including John Hancock.

ask for recognition by foreign governments. Still, the Continental Army faced an almost impossible task in fighting against the formidable military of the British Empire, which controlled New York City and by 1777 even took Philadelphia, leading General Washington into retreat at Valley Forge. Also in late 1777, however, the Continental Army won the critical battle of Saratoga in upstate New York, disrupting the British plan to divide and conquer the colonies.

By 1778, the French government officially recognized the United States of America, allowing foreign aid, supplies and military advisers from mainland Europe to arrive and help the Continental Army. This assistance helped the outcome of the war, and after several key battles, the British surrendered at the Battle of Yorktown in October 1781. The Treaty of Paris officially ended the war in 1783.

George Washington resigned his commission and retired to Mount Vernon, but a grassroots effort to recruit him for president convinced him. On April 6, 1789, Congress declared Washington the first president of the United States, with John Adams as his vice president. And the next four presidents were all Founding Fathers: John Adams, Thomas Jefferson, James Madison and James Monroe.

GEORGE
WASHINGTON

AFTER DEFEATING THE BRITISH, WASHINGTON BECAME THE UNANIMOUS CHOICE TO GUIDE THE NEWLY FORMED NATION

★ ★ ★

RANKING
2

GEORGE WASHINGTON, WHO HAD NO MIDDLE NAME, began his military career in the Virginia Militia, part of the defense system set up by the British to protect their colonies, and distinguished himself fighting the French. Eventually, and more famously, he became the commander in chief of the Continental Army that won the American Revolutionary War. At the onset of the war, Washington lamented to American statesman Richard Henry Lee, "Between you and me, I think we are in an exceedingly dangerous situation." Fought bitterly and at times desperately between 1775 and 1783, the originally lopsided conflict between the professional, experienced British army and the mostly inexperienced, cobbled-together patriots established Washington as one of the greatest military leaders of modern —not just American—history.

He remains the only U.S. president elected unanimously, winning 69 out of 69 Electoral College votes representing the then 10 states;

KEY ACHIEVEMENTS

- Signed the Naturalization Act of 1790 and the Slave Trade Act of 1794.

- Created the United States Mint and the first bank.

- The only Founding Father to free his slaves.

- Established Cabinet positions.

he was also reelected unanimously in 1793. (In 1820, James Monroe won 231 out of 232 Electoral College votes—the lone holdout, New Hampshire elector William Plumer, is said to have done so in order to preserve Washington's perfect record, but the truth is that Plumer thought Monroe was a weak president and that John Quincy Adams would be a better choice.)

Washington's presidency, being the first, naturally established a number of institutional precedents, something to which he was particularly sensitive. As he explained in a letter to fellow Founding Father (and future president) James Madison: "It is devoutly wished on my part that these precedents be fixed on true principles." Washington began the traditions of an inaugural address, which subtly distinguished his inauguration from a coronation, as well as an annual message to Congress that grew into the State of the Union. He also created the concept of a Cabinet for his administration. With great foresight he insisted on being addressed as

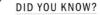

DID YOU KNOW?
Washington's second inaugural address was under two minutes long and contained only 135 words.

"TO BE PREPARED FOR WAR IS ONE OF THE MOST EFFECTUAL MEANS OF PRESERVING PEACE." GEORGE WASHINGTON

The National Portrait Gallery has 146 portraits of Washington in its collection.

WASHINGTON'S TOP FIVE BATTLES

Washington and his troops rode through the city after the Siege of Boston in 1775.

The Siege of Boston

This was a stunning victory for the Continental Army, taking a massively important British stronghold. In November 1775, Washington guided recently captured cannons to the top of Dorchester Hills, from where his group of farmers and laborers with little training sunk British ships. The British commander retreated to Nova Scotia.

The Battle of Harlem Heights

After losing New York to the British in his worst defeat of the war, Washington pulled his troops north to Harlem Heights in September 1776. General Howe's forces initially pushed the Continental force back, before a flank attack defeated the British.

Trenton

Early on December 26, 1776, Washington's troops spent a freezing, all-around miserable night crossing the Delaware River from Pennsylvania and attacked the British fort. They surprised the enemy and forced a relatively quick surrender, taking over Trenton.

Valley Forge and the Battle of Monmouth

In December 1777, Washington's army camped in Valley Forge, Pennsylvania, and over the harsh winter he honed them into a superb fighting force. In a sense, turning his soldiers—worn out, hungry and disconsolate from a string of defeats—into a disciplined and sharper army was Washington's hardest battle and his greatest triumph. In June 1778, Washington's troops attacked and severely weakened the British in Monmouth, New Jersey, as they were coming north from Philadelphia, which the Redcoats had captured the previous year. In regard to Washington's service at Monmouth, the Marquis de Lafayette recalled, "I had never beheld so superb a man."

The Siege of Yorktown

In the late summer of 1781, British General Cornwallis encamped his force in Yorktown, Virginia, with the plan of waiting for reinforcements before moving to British-controlled New York. Washington, with his French allies, pounced, capturing key territory, and by October Cornwallis surrendered.

Mr. President rather than the grander honorifics Congress wanted to call him, like His Highness the President. And he created Thanksgiving.

Washington inherited a weak and troubled post-Revolutionary War government that had large debts, an unmoored monetary system and poor structure. But he also had Alexander Hamilton as Secretary of Treasury , whose vision for economic stability led to the birth of the First Bank of the United States.

Washington was the first president to try to abolish slavery, but it was an effort that failed when Georgia and South Carolina threatened civil war.

He would have retired after his first term, but decided to continue in order to mitigate the potentially country-splitting political infighting in his government, particularly between Secretary of State Thomas Jefferson and Hamilton. However, we have Jefferson and Hamilton to thank for creating the two-party system, making Washington the only president to not be affiliated with a political party.

And Washington was ahead of his time in his (mostly) sensitive dealings with Native Americans, at first opposing the seemingly inexorable confiscation of their land and resettling of tribes. He decried that "frontier settlers entertain the opinion that there is not the same crime (or indeed no crime at all) in killing an Indian as in killing a white man." He convened a meeting with two dozen tribes in New York, where he magnanimously dealt with the tribal leaders as equals—revolutionary at the time—and arrived at a treaty that would give them land and farming supplies. Unfortunately, angered by a number of slaughters of American troops and settlers by Native Americans, he later authorized his army to drive tribes farther west by burning their villages and crops.

At the end of his second term he declared that he would not run for a third, stemming partly from a desire to retire and partly from a sense that this nascent democracy he helped create should have new leaders, rather than risk even the slightest chance of lapsing into anything resembling a monarchy.

Less than three years after he left the presidency, Washington died at the age of 67 in his Mount Vernon home in Virginia, now a museum. In his final years he worked managing his five contiguous farms. Even more tiring, he received an apparently endless amount of visitors who would turn up, basically, just to meet the father of the country. This selfless life led him to being described by historian Ron Chernow as "the most famously elusive figure in American history."

Washington's death was a medieval case of medical mismanagement. In December 1799, just under three weeks from fulfilling his long-standing prediction that he would live to see the next century, he got drenched with rain while making the rounds of his property and arrived

1789–1797

BORN FEB. 22, 1732, POPE'S CREEK, WESTMORELAND COUNTY, VIRGINIA
DIED DEC. 14, 1799, MOUNT VERNON, VIRGINIA
BURIAL SITE WASHINGTON BURIAL VAULT, MOUNT VERNON, VIRGINIA
EDUCATION PRIVATE TUTORS
POLITICAL PARTY FEDERALIST
AGE AT INAUGURATION 57
VICE PRESIDENT JOHN ADAMS
OPPONENTS NONE, ELECTED UNANIMOUSLY (1ST TERM); JOHN ADAMS (2ND TERM)
OCCUPATIONS BEFORE PRESIDENCY SURVEYOR, PLANTER, GENERAL
OTHER OFFICES MEMBER OF VIRGINIA HOUSE OF BURGESSES; MEMBER OF CONTINENTAL CONGRESS; CHAIRMAN OF CONSTITUTIONAL CONVENTION
FIRST LADY MARTHA CUSTIS WASHINGTON
NICKNAMES OLD MAN, THE FATHER OF HIS COUNTRY, THE AMERICAN CINCINNATUS

home to find his dinner guests already seated. He chose not to change out of his wet clothes, and then went out again the next day, which got him even more sick. The following day, bedridden, he was attended to by a series of inept doctors, who bled him repeatedly, almost choked him to death with a preparation of molasses, butter and vinegar, and probably finished the poor man off when they scalded his throat with a toxic tincture on the inspired notion of further blistering his swollen, probably infected throat to help relieve it.

On his deathbed, before uttering his final words, "Tis well" to personal secretary Tobias Lear, Washington expressed the fear—not entirely irrational in those days—of being buried alive, so he was kept in the house's vault for three days after his death on December 14. He was finally interred on his estate seven days before Christmas.

By the end of his presidency, Washington came to know the bitter taste of efforts by his political enemies to discredit and undermine him, and of the press accusing him (falsely) of profiteering. In his farewell address—which is considered alongside the Gettysburg Address as one of the great American speeches—he declared that national unity was essential in order to preserve freedom and prosperity. And, presciently, he warned of three great dangers to the Republic: regionalism, political tribalism and foreign entanglements. Perhaps America's greatest leader and statesman left the stage he so influentially helped build at exactly the right time.

WHATEVER HAPPENED TO THE FEDERALIST PARTY?

Naval officer Oliver Hazard Perry (standing) is depicted at the Battle of Lake Erie in the War of 1812.

In the beginning, the Federalist Party was more an ideology and an abstract concept than a political party. For a start, there was no other party—so there wasn't that dynamic of wrestling for supremacy and installing of candidates, until the endless feud between Thomas Jefferson and Alexander Hamilton made Republicans and Federalists the first American political tribes. The Federalists were the framers of the Constitution. They believed in liberty and a strong central government, while fearing the choke hold a strong federal government could have over liberties. Federalism, at its heart, was neurotic. But that's not what killed it: The War of 1812 did. The war against the British severely impacted the economy of the Northeast states, where the Federalists were strongest, and led to talk of secession to get out of the war and back to trading with Europe. When the war turned and the U.S. finally routed the British, the Federalists were seen as unpatriotic and self-interested, and from then on the party was considered too unpopular to survive.

BY GEORGE!
Washington is sworn in as the nation's first president at Federal Hall in New York City.

JOHN ADAMS

HIS LIFELONG DEDICATION TO THE PURSUIT OF LIBERTY IS BELIEVED TO BE HIS GREATEST LEGACY, FAR SURPASSING ADAMS' ACHIEVEMENTS AS U.S. PRESIDENT

★ ★ ☆

RANKING
16

BY THE TIME JOHN ADAMS WAS ELECTED THE SECOND president of the United States, defeating Thomas Jefferson by just three electoral votes, the Harvard-educated lawyer was already well known for his bold opposition to British rule over the American colonies and had forged a career noted for the pursuit of America's freedom. Because of his early fervent and outspoken dedication to the importance of freedom and liberty, Adams became part of the five-person committee that conceived the Declaration of Independence during the summer of 1776. It was Adams who nominated Jefferson, his future vice president turned adversary, to draft the document.

After attending the Continental Congress as a delegate in the 1770s, he later served as a European diplomat, helping to negotiate the Treaty of Paris, which formally ended the American Revolutionary War in 1783. After the war, Adams was the first U.S. Ambassador to Britain, from 1785–1788. Upon returning to America, he participated

KEY ACHIEVEMENTS

- Opposed the 1765 Stamp Act, which imposed taxation on the British colonies in America.

- Helped negotiate the Treaty of Paris, which officially ended the Revolutionary War.

- Part of the committee responsible for the Declaration of Independence.

in securing George Washington the nomination for the first United States presidency, and became America's first vice president. But the eight years Adams spent as Washington's No. 2 (1789–1797) were not, by Adams' standards, productive ones. While Washington took to the forefront, Adams was known to refer to his VP role as "insignificant": "My country has in its wisdom contrived for me the most insignificant office that ever the invention of man contrived or his imagination conceived."

At the time of Adams' presidency, Britain and France were at war. The French Foreign Minister refused to deal with Adams' delegate—demanding a large bribe. Adams rejected this idea and in 1798, an undeclared war broke out between America and France until a peace treaty ended it in 1800.

Adams lost his campaign for a second term, likely due to Jefferson's paid propaganda against him and his character—the first negative presidential campaign. Jefferson called Adams

DID YOU KNOW?
Adams was the first president to live in the original White House, designed by architect James Hoban, taking residence in November 1800.

Adams was a direct descendant of Puritan colonists who settled in Massachusetts.

"Writing the Declaration of Independence," by Jean Leon Gerome Ferris, commemorates the founders' important work.

"distrustful, obstinate, excessively vain, and takes no counsel from anyone." The lies included stories about Adams smuggling British prostitutes into America and unsubstantiated claims that Adams was planning to marry one of his sons into British royalty. But it worked, and Adams was defeated by his own vice president in 1801.

Adams, who was known for his strong moral compass and his refusal to accept bribes or play into political favoritism, was a symbol of integrity. However, historians Joanne Freeman and Douglas Ambrose have called his presidency "unsuccessful," although both credit Adams with staying out of a full-scale war with France. According to Freeman, Adams declared this to be one of his greatest achievements in an otherwise non-stellar presidency.

After his presidency, Adams retired to the same town where he was born—now split into two towns, with his locale renamed Quincy after his wife Abigail's maternal grandfather, Col. John Quincy. The last years of Adams' life were devoted to his prolific writing, most notably an exchange of letters with Jefferson, with whom he was now reconciled. Ambrose described them as "witty, often profound, and always revealing" and that they displayed "their wonderfully self-conscious and always interesting reflections about the era and their roles in it."

Adams also famously exchanged more than 1,100 letters with Abigail that were written throughout his life and career. Most survived, and they serve as a first-person account of American history. They speak to his deep devotion as a husband and father to their six children. Further, it was intellectual, feminist-for-her-time Abigail—often referred to as "Mrs. President"—who famously urged her husband to "remember the ladies" when considering the future of American citizens.

Two years after his son John Quincy Adams was elected in 1824, Adams passed away of congestive heart failure. His last words were said to be: "Thomas Jefferson survives," not knowing that Jefferson had passed away that morning. They both died on July 4, 1826, 50 years to the day after they signed the Declaration of Independence together.

"TO BE GOOD, AND TO DO GOOD, IS ALL WE HAVE TO DO."

JOHN ADAMS

1797–1801

BORN OCT. 30, 1735, BRAINTREE, MASSACHUSETTS
DIED JULY 4, 1826, QUINCY, MASSACHUSETTS
BURIAL SITE FIRST UNITARIAN CHURCH, QUINCY, MASSACHUSETTS
EDUCATION HARVARD UNIVERSITY
POLITICAL PARTY FEDERALIST
AGE AT INAUGURATION 61
VICE PRESIDENT THOMAS JEFFERSON
OPPONENT THOMAS JEFFERSON
OCCUPATIONS BEFORE PRESIDENCY TEACHER, FARMER, LAWYER, SURVEYOR, SELECTMAN
OTHER OFFICES REPRESENTATIVE TO MASSACHUSETTS GENERAL COURT; DELEGATE TO FIRST AND SECOND CONTINENTAL CONGRESSES; MEMBER OF PROVINCIAL CONGRESS OF MASSACHUSETTS; DELEGATE TO MASSACHUSETTS CONSTITUTIONAL CONVENTION; COMMISSIONER TO FRANCE; MINISTER TO NETHERLANDS AND BRITAIN; U.S. VICE PRESIDENT
FIRST LADY ABIGAIL SMITH ADAMS
NICKNAMES ATLAS OF INDEPENDENCE, DUKE OF BRAINTREE, HIS ROTUNDITY, OLD SINK OR SWIM, THE COLOSSUS OF INDEPENDENCE

THOMAS
JEFFERSON

HAVING THE SKILLS FOR MANY CAREERS, JEFFERSON DECLARED WRITING WAS ONE OF HIS MOST POWERFUL

★ ★ ★

RANKING

4

A PROLIFIC WRITER BUT BY MANY HISTORICAL ACCOUNTS a reluctant orator, Thomas Jefferson was elected as the Virginia delegate to the Second Continental Congress in Philadelphia in 1776. It was there that Jefferson was tapped to write the first draft of a declaration that outlined the causes of the American Revolution. His words, "We hold these truths to be self-evident, that all men are created equal, that they are endowed by their Creator with certain unalienable Rights, that among these are Life, Liberty and the pursuit of Happiness," echo through the ages as the most famous discourse on human rights.

Following the death of his beloved wife, Martha, the widowed Jefferson shipped off to Europe to follow in the footsteps of elder statesman Benjamin Franklin as American minister to France. He served as the first Secretary of State under George Washington from 1790 to 1793. After Washington declined a third presidential term, Jefferson ushered in our two-party system with his leadership of the nation's first opposition political party, known as the Democratic-Republican party (opposite Alexander Hamilton's Federalist party). In the election of 1800, Jefferson overwhelmingly defeated John Adams to become the third president of the United States.

In his inaugural address, Jefferson, who held strict constructionist views, advocated for limited federal government and the rights of states. His foreign policy was dictated by his intention to seek "peace, commerce, and honest friendship with all nations—entangling alliances with none." Shortly into his first term, Jefferson got into a mighty tangle with the pasha of Tripoli when he refused to make ransom payments to Barbary pirates in order to conduct trade through the Mediterranean. He sent a naval squadron to the region and the first of the Barbary Wars began. Historian Dave Benner points out that "while the engagements with the Barbary powers continued intermittently throughout the next few years, Jefferson's diligence paid off in the end."

In 1802, Jefferson established the United States Military Academy at West Point. But it was a Constitutional gamble that he took in direct response to an alarming act of Spain in October of

KEY ACHIEVEMENTS

- Wrote the Declaration of Independence.
- Doubled the size of the U.S. by acquiring the entire Louisiana Territory.
- Sent Lewis and Clark to explore west of the Mississippi River.
- Banned slave trading.

DID YOU KNOW?

Jefferson was also an inventor. Among his creations: a macaroni machine, swivel chairs and the "polygraph"— a machine that duplicated an original document as it was being created.

"THE PRINCIPLES OF JEFFERSON ARE THE AXIOMS OF A FREE SOCIETY." ABRAHAM LINCOLN

Jefferson was the first president to be inaugurated in Washington, D.C.

1802 that would prove Jefferson's greatness as a visionary leader.

After Spain began banning American ships from delivering goods to the Port of New Orleans—a port that was critical to American commerce—Jefferson, armed with the knowledge that Spain had secretly retroceded the Louisiana territory back to France, directed then-minister to France Robert Livingston to negotiate for land on the Lower Mississippi River. Jefferson wrote Livingston: "Every eye in the U.S.

is now fixed on this affair of Louisiana. Perhaps nothing since the Revolutionary War has produced more uneasy sensations through the body of the nation." Negotiations ensued and by the end of April 1803 the Louisiana Purchase was completed. Nowhere in the Constitution, which came into force in 1789, did it provide for such grand executive powers to purchase land, so Jefferson drafted an amendment that would authorize the purchase of Louisiana retroactively. Congress ultimately

HOW DID JEFFERSON TRULY FEEL ABOUT SLAVERY?

CONTRADICTIONS ABOUND ON THE PRESIDENT'S MORAL STANCE

A vocal opponent against the international slave trade, Thomas Jefferson took to task the British king for allowing the "execrable commerce" of slavery to continue. Worded as a separate paragraph in the Declaration of Independence, Jefferson's denouncement was later omitted in the final draft.

Contrarily, Jefferson profited off owning slaves his entire life. While he drafted laws and was involved in legislation that supported the abolishment of slavery, he also held a common view of blacks in his day, as expressed in his writings from Notes on The State of Virginia, "comparing them by their faculties of memory, reason, and imagination, it appears to me that in memory they are equal to the whites; in reason much inferior."

Jefferson's relationship with Sally Hemings, the half-sister of his late wife, and a slave in the Jefferson household, first entered the public consciousness during his first term as president and had long been fodder for political ammunition from his opponents. According to various accounts throughout the last two centuries, Jefferson fathered six of her children. The Thomas Jefferson Foundation settled the historical matter in an official statement that corroborates numerous oral and documentary accounts through history, along with the results of a DNA study published in 1998, that showed the male-line descendants of Sally Heming's son, Eston, and Jefferson's grandfather shared the same Y-chromosome haplotype, and said they will no longer use qualifying language when discussing the paternity of Sally Heming's children.

While he held a position against slavery, Jefferson still made use of slaves on his estate.

Jefferson was only 33 years old when he was asked to write the Declaration of Independence.

"I BELIEVE THAT EVERY HUMAN MIND FEELS PLEASURE IN DOING GOOD TO ANOTHER." THOMAS JEFFERSON

Explorers Meriwether Lewis and William Clark covered nearly 8,000 miles on their expedition.

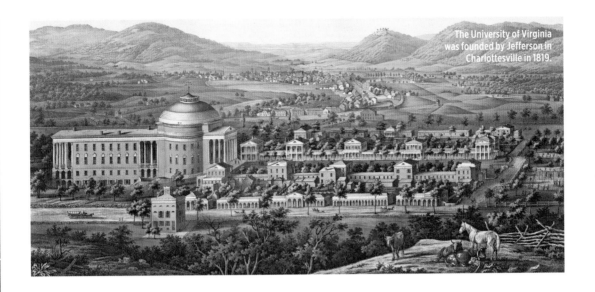

The University of Virginia was founded by Jefferson in Charlottesville in 1819.

1801–1809

BORN APRIL 13, 1743, GOOCHLAND (NOW ALBEMARLE) COUNTY, VIRGINIA
DIED JULY 4, 1826, MONTICELLO, CHARLOTTESVILLE, VIRGINIA
BURIAL SITE MONTICELLO, CHARLOTTESVILLE, VIRGINIA
EDUCATION COLLEGE OF WILLIAM & MARY
POLITICAL PARTY DEMOCRATIC-REPUBLICAN
AGE AT INAUGURATION 57
VICE PRESIDENTS AARON BURR (1ST TERM); GEORGE CLINTON (2ND TERM)
OPPONENTS AARON BURR (1ST TERM); CHARLES C. PINCKNEY (2ND TERM)
OCCUPATIONS BEFORE PRESIDENCY PLANTER, LAWYER, WRITER, PHILOSOPHER, SCIENTIST, ARCHITECT
OTHER OFFICES MEMBER OF VIRGINIA HOUSE OF BURGESSES; COUNTY LIEUTENANT; COUNTY SURVEYOR; DEPUTY DELEGATE TO SECOND CONTINENTAL CONGRESS; MEMBER OF VIRGINIA HOUSE OF DELEGATES; GOVERNOR OF VIRGINIA; COMMISSIONER TO FRANCE; MINISTER TO FRANCE; SECRETARY OF STATE; U.S. VICE PRESIDENT
FIRST LADY MARTHA WAYLES SKELTON JEFFERSON
NICKNAME THE RED FOX

disregarded his draft, and the Senate ratified the treaty with France in October of 1803.

Historians Robert E. Wright and David Cowen pointed out the "upstart nation" acquired land physically larger than France, Spain, Portugal, Italy, Holland, Switzerland and the British Isles combined, practically overnight. And in August of 1803, Jefferson had commissioned Meriwether Lewis, who chose William Clark as his co-leader, to lead an expedition to explore and report on the vast and uncharted territory, immortalizing the land purchase as one of Jefferson's greatest accomplishments in office.

Jefferson was elected to a second term that was marked by his controversial and economically devastating Embargo Act of 1807, which prevented U.S. ships from any trade with Europe. Jefferson believed that dependence on American goods would force France and England to honor American neutrality. It backfired.

In addition to his place in history as a Founding Father, Jefferson continued his mission of nurturing the University of Virginia, the college he founded, until the time of his death on July 4, 1826—exactly 50 years to the day that the nation formally declared its independence.

JAMES MADISON

THE ARCHITECT OF THE CONSTITUTION FORMED THE FOUNDATION OF DEMOCRACY, YET HIS PRESIDENCY WAS DOMINATED BY ANOTHER WAR WITH GREAT BRITAIN

★ ★ ☆

RANKING 13

JAMES MADISON, A TITAN AMONG THE THINK-TANK of geniuses known collectively as the Founding Fathers, outlined the principles of a strong national government at the Constitutional Convention of New York in 1787. His ideas of government structure was a three-branch system: a separation of power held by Congress (legislative), the office of the president (executive) and a federal court system (judicial). Humble and quick to point out that it was the "work of many heads and many hands," nonetheless, his brilliant outline formed the basis of democracy and earned him the moniker "Father of the Constitution."

Born into a prominent family of Virginia planters, much like his colleague Thomas Jefferson, Madison had a keen intellect and studied philosophy and theology, Greek and Latin at what is now Princeton University. He first entered politics as a representative to the Virginia Constitutional Convention during the Revolutionary War, moving into national politics in 1780 when he was elected to the Continental Congress, where he hoped to shore up what he viewed as a weak national government.

KEY ACHIEVEMENTS

• Battled Great Britain in the War of 1812, which lead to prosperity and national pride.

• Passed the Tariff of 1816 to protect U.S. manufactured items from overseas competition.

• Signed a bill rechartering a new national bank in Philadelphia.

By 1787, he had helped plan the Constitutional Convention, where his ideas for the Virginia Constitution were developed into what became the U.S. document, and Madison joined Alexander Hamilton and John Jay in writing the Federalist Papers, a series of essays promoting the ratification of the new Constitution, which was approved by all of the states in 1789.

While the country had enjoyed over two decades of peace, Madison was elected president in 1808 during a time of conflict between Britain and France (led by Napoleon) that impacted American trade. Both countries seized U.S. cargo as the ships were bound for each other's shores. France soon bowed to Madison's demands to stop the practice. But Britain refused to recognize the young United States' maritime rights and its identity as a neutral nation and continued enforcing its naval blockade, capturing, beating and impressing American seaman by forcing them to join the British Naval Army. Additionally, British military supported Native Americans, who posed a threat to the desired expansion of U.S. territory.

DID YOU KNOW?

The scar on Madison's nose is from frostbite he suffered during a long ride home after a debate with James Monroe in 1788.

Eight U.S. presidents, including Madison, have been from Virginia—the most from any state.

29

The U.S. had an important victory over Britain in the War of 1812's Battle of Lake Erie.

"THE TRUTH IS THAT ALL MEN HAVING POWER OUGHT TO BE MISTRUSTED."

JAMES MADISON

While he expounded on the virtues of diplomacy in his first inaugural address to "cherish peace and friendly intercourse with all nations having correspondent dispositions," Madison's war message to Congress listed Great Britain's numerous transgressions against the U.S., and with Congress' approval—and the first time in the 25-year history of the young country—Madison exercised the power to declare war.

On June 18, 1812, an unprepared United States entered war with Britain, much to popular dissatisfaction. Still, Madison's naysayers expressed themselves without fear of treason charges or imprisonment— a testament to the strength of the Constitution and Americans' rights to freedom of speech.

For three years, the U.S. fought the British in bloody battles in New Orleans and across British territories in Canada. On September 10, 1813, the largest naval battle of the war was fought on Lake Erie, where the American navy defeated and captured six British Royal Navy ships. But the nation suffered a symbolic blow on August 24,

1814, when the British captured and burned the capital in Washington, D.C. (Madison's vivacious wife, Dolley, whose style and presence is credited with enhancing Madison's image, saved the full-length portrait of George Washington that still hangs in the White House today.) It was the first time since the Revolutionary War that a foreign power had occupied our country's capital.

With Napoleon's defeat in 1814, the British public grew tired of the expense of war. Following the failure of an assault on Baltimore, the British entered into The Treaty of Ghent with the U.S. The war officially ended on December 24, 1814, securing the frontier north of the Ohio River and west of the Mississippi River for settlement by the U.S.

The War of 1812 is often seen as declaration of national honor and pride in the face of a powerful Great Britain, and historians often refer to it as the United States' "Second War of Independence." Madison's second term in office has been dubbed "The Era of Good Feelings," characterized by national unity and a pause, if not an end, to bitter partisan politics, as a sense of patriotism rose. He left office a popular and beloved figure and retired to his tobacco plantation, Montpelier, in 1817. Former president John Adams wrote to Thomas Jefferson that year, saying of Madison, "his Administration acquired more glory, and established more Union, than all his three predecessors, Washington, Adams, and Jefferson, put together."

1809–1817

BORN MARCH 16, 1751, PORT CONWAY, VIRGINIA
DIED JUNE 28, 1836, MONTPELIER, VIRGINIA
BURIAL SITE MADISON FAMILY CEMETERY, MONTPELIER, VIRGINIA
EDUCATION COLLEGE OF NEW JERSEY (NOW PRINCETON UNIVERSITY)
POLITICAL PARTY DEMOCRATIC-REPUBLICAN
AGE AT INAUGURATION 57
VICE PRESIDENTS GEORGE CLINTON (1ST TERM); ELBRIDGE GERRY (2ND TERM)
OPPONENTS CHARLES C. PINCKNEY (1ST TERM); DEWITT CLINTON (2ND TERM)
OCCUPATION BEFORE PRESIDENCY POLITICIAN
OTHER OFFICES MEMBER OF CONTINENTAL CONGRESS; MEMBER OF VIRGINIA LEGISLATURE; MEMBER OF CONSTITUTIONAL CONVENTION; MEMBER OF U.S. HOUSE OF REPRESENTATIVES; SECRETARY OF STATE
FIRST LADY DOROTHEA (DOLLEY) PAYNE TODD MADISON
NICKNAMES THE FATHER OF THE CONSTITUTION, LITTLE JEMMY

Dolley Madison was 17 years younger than her husband.

JAMES
MONROE

THE EXPERIENCED MONROE SET FORTH
THE UNITED STATES' FIRST FOREIGN POLICY

★ ★ ★

RANKING
15

SKILLFUL FOREIGN POLICY WAS A HALLMARK OF FOUNDING Father James Monroe's presidency. His most recognizable achievement, the Monroe Doctrine, was a critical piece of legislature that changed how America viewed the world, and how the rest of the world viewed America.

Based on the ideas of Secretary of State John Quincy Adams, the Monroe Doctrine effectively states four key points: 1) the United States' political system is separate from the European system; 2) the U.S. will no longer be colonized by Europe; 3) the U.S. has the right to oppose any European colonization (or recolonization for that matter) of independent republics in the Americas; and 4) the U.S. will respect and not interfere in any and all established European colonies in the Americas or become involved with Europe's domestic affairs or intervene in any European wars that do not impact the U.S.

Monroe did reject Adams' idea to first inform other nations of the new U.S. policy. Instead, Monroe announced it to Congress in his State of the Union Address of 1823: "It is impossible that the allied powers should extend their political system to any portion of either continent without endangering our peace and happiness."

The fear of recolonization of Latin America by European monarchs led to wide support of the Monroe Doctrine when it was presented. Over time, sitting presidents, like Theodore Roosevelt, have used it to enact various policies throughout the Americas, proving it to be a powerful and resilient tool of American foreign policy.

Monroe, described by historian John M. Taylor as being "workmanlike" and "less scholarly than his presidential predecessors, and lacking charisma," was the only person to have held two cabinet positions (Secretary of War and Secretary of State) at the same time, when serving under President James Madison. The quiet and capable Virginian decided to fill his own cabinet with members who were geographically spread out. His appointments of northerner John Quincy Adams (Secretary of State), and southerner John C. Calhoun (Secretary of War) eased political tensions at the time. Also in his first term, Monroe, who was the last president to wear the fashions of the 18th

KEY ACHIEVEMENTS

- Articulated the Monroe Doctrine, the country's first foreign policy.

- Improved relations with the U.K. and Canada, signing the Treaty of 1818.

- Recognized new Latin American countries as independent.

- Helped negotiate the Louisiana Purchase, nearly doubling the size of the country.

- The only person to serve two cabinet positions at once: Secretary of State and Secretary of War.

Monroe served key positions in two administrations before taking office as president.

DID YOU KNOW?

The African country Liberia, founded as a refuge for freed slaves, named its capital Monrovia after Monroe helped procure funds to acquire the land.

"MONROE WAS SO HONEST THAT IF YOU TURNED HIS SOUL INSIDE OUT THERE WOULD NOT BE A SPOT ON IT." THOMAS JEFFERSON

DID YOU KNOW?
In the famous painting "Washington Crossing the Delaware," it is Monroe who is depicted standing behind George Washington and holding the flag.

century (powdered wig, knee breeches, long white stockings, buckled shoes), went on a goodwill tour in 1817, visiting as far west as Michigan and the Missouri territory, as far north as Maine, and south to Georgia and Kentucky. After visiting Boston on the tour, the *Columbian Centinel* newspaper proclaimed this to be the "Era of Good Feelings"— a term the nation got behind for the next decade.

Prior to becoming president, Monroe had been sent to France by his friend and political ally Thomas Jefferson to help negotiate the Louisiana Purchase. The resulting land deal between the United States and France helped the country eventually acquire approximately 827,000 square miles of land west of the Mississippi River for $15 million. (Napoleon changed his mind on the initial terms of the U.S.

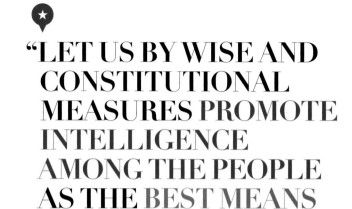

"LET US BY WISE AND CONSTITUTIONAL MEASURES PROMOTE INTELLIGENCE AMONG THE PEOPLE AS THE BEST MEANS OF PRESERVING OUR LIBERTIES." JAMES MONROE

1817–1825

BORN APRIL 28, 1758, WESTMORELAND COUNTY, VIRGINIA
DIED JULY 4, 1831, NEW YORK, NEW YORK
BURIAL SITE HOLLYWOOD CEMETERY, RICHMOND, VIRGINIA
EDUCATION COLLEGE OF WILLIAM AND MARY
POLITICAL PARTY DEMOCRATIC-REPUBLICAN
AGE AT INAUGURATION 58
VICE PRESIDENT DANIEL D. TOMPKINS
OPPONENTS RUFUS KING (1ST TERM); NONE, RAN UNOPPOSED (2ND TERM)
OCCUPATION BEFORE PRESIDENCY LAWYER
OTHER OFFICES MILITARY COMMISSIONER FOR SOUTHERN ARMY; REPRESENTATIVE TO VIRGINIA LEGISLATURE, VIRGINIA ASSEMBLY; MEMBER OF GOVERNOR JEFFERSON'S COUNCIL; REPRESENTATIVE TO VIRGINIA HOUSE OF DELEGATES; REPRESENTATIVE AT CONTINENTAL CONGRESS; U.S. SENATOR; MINISTER TO FRANCE AND ENGLAND; GOVERNOR OF VIRGINIA; SECRETARY OF STATE; SECRETARY OF WAR
FIRST LADY ELIZABETH KORTRIGHT MONROE
NICKNAMES THE LAST COCKED HAT, ERA-OF-GOOD-FEELINGS PRESIDENT

purchasing only New Orleans and all or part of Florida for $10 million.) Jefferson had the utmost confidence in Monroe but added some pressure, telling him "all eyes, all hopes, are now fixed on you...for on the event of this mission depends the future destinies of this republic." The official announcement of the purchase was made July 4, 1803. Monroe died 28 years later, on July 4, 1831.

JOHN QUINCY
ADAMS

*HIS MOST REMARKABLE ACHIEVEMENTS
WEREN'T ACTUALLY DURING HIS PRESIDENCY*

★ ★ ★

RANKING
20

AS PRESIDENT, JOHN QUINCY ADAMS WAS FAIRLY
unremarkable. To begin, he wasn't even elected,
being one of the few presidents to take the oath of
office without it being the express will of the people,
who may have taken his comment about voting too
seriously: "Always vote for principle, though you
may vote alone."

Adams grew up well-versed in the importance
of individual liberties. As the
eldest son of Founding Father
John Adams, he was appointed
ambassador to the Netherlands by
George Washington when he was
just 26, launching his career as one
of the great American diplomats.
"From the experience of the past we
derive instructive lessons for the
future," he noted. In 1814, Adams
was asked to help negotiate a peace
treaty between the U.S. and the
U.K. following the War of 1812.
The subsequent Treaty of Ghent
ushered in more than two centuries
of peace between the two nations.

Adams was named James Monroe's Secretary of
State in 1817. His first achievement was the Treaty
of 1818, also between the U.S. and the U.K., which
established boundaries over America's Pacific

**KEY
ACHIEVEMENTS**

• Oversaw the completion
of the Erie Canal;
gave funding to the
construction of the
Chesapeake and Ohio
Canal (C&O Canal).

• Negotiated the
acquisition of Florida
and Oregon from Spain.

Although he earned
a master's degree
from Harvard, Adams
became a lawyer
wihout ever attending
law school.

Northwest territory. His influence was felt again when Monroe laid out the tenets of the Monroe Doctrine, much of which Adams himself helped to craft. Shifting American international interests away from Europe and toward the Americas, it laid the foundation for U.S. foreign policy in the years ahead.

In 1824, no candidate won a majority, although Andrew Jackson won the popular vote. Congress was called upon to decide the election and chose Adams. Members of that same Congress who supported Jackson took their revenge by blocking Adams' initiatives for building infrastructure and expanding education, preventing him from having any major policy successes. He did manage to secure a number

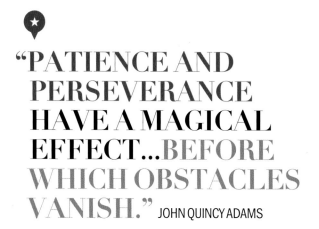

DID YOU KNOW?
Adams often woke up at 5:00 a.m. to go skinny-dipping in the Potomac River as a form of exercise.

of treaties with other countries, but in 1828 he lost reelection to Jackson in a landslide.

After serving just one term, Adams went on to become the only ex-president to continue in government, serving in the House of Representatives for nine terms. In the 1830s, abolitionists repeatedly petitioned the House of Representatives to end slavery, but Southern House members passed a "gag rule" that tabled all appeals on it. Adams, who wasn't an abolitionist, felt that any person who wanted to petition had a right that "belongs to humanity." His impassioned arguments in the historic Amistad trial in 1840, where kidnapped Africans on a slave ship were fighting for their freedom, helped cement his reputation as a vehement spokesman for individual rights. And his fight for civil liberties led to the "gag rule" being overturned in 1844.

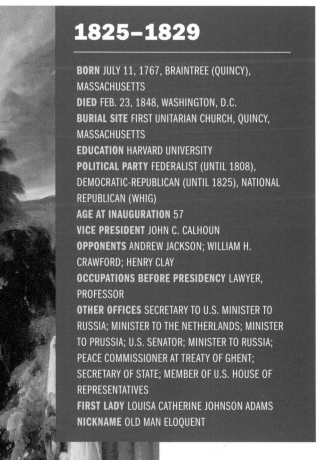

1825–1829

BORN JULY 11, 1767, BRAINTREE (QUINCY), MASSACHUSETTS
DIED FEB. 23, 1848, WASHINGTON, D.C.
BURIAL SITE FIRST UNITARIAN CHURCH, QUINCY, MASSACHUSETTS
EDUCATION HARVARD UNIVERSITY
POLITICAL PARTY FEDERALIST (UNTIL 1808), DEMOCRATIC-REPUBLICAN (UNTIL 1825), NATIONAL REPUBLICAN (WHIG)
AGE AT INAUGURATION 57
VICE PRESIDENT JOHN C. CALHOUN
OPPONENTS ANDREW JACKSON; WILLIAM H. CRAWFORD; HENRY CLAY
OCCUPATIONS BEFORE PRESIDENCY LAWYER, PROFESSOR
OTHER OFFICES SECRETARY TO U.S. MINISTER TO RUSSIA; MINISTER TO THE NETHERLANDS; MINISTER TO PRUSSIA; U.S. SENATOR; MINISTER TO RUSSIA; PEACE COMMISSIONER AT TREATY OF GHENT; SECRETARY OF STATE; MEMBER OF U.S. HOUSE OF REPRESENTATIVES
FIRST LADY LOUISA CATHERINE JOHNSON ADAMS
NICKNAME OLD MAN ELOQUENT

"PATIENCE AND PERSEVERANCE HAVE A MAGICAL EFFECT...BEFORE WHICH OBSTACLES VANISH." JOHN QUINCY ADAMS

HISTORY OF THE
WHITE HOUSE

*THE PRESIDENT'S HOME HAS BEEN BURNED DOWN,
IT'S HAUNTED...AND IT'S NOT EVEN WHITE*

★ ★ ☆

THE FIRST THING YOU NEED TO KNOW ABOUT THE WHITE
House is that it was originally called—and was
intended to be—the People's House.

That seems quaint and innocent and slightly
ridiculous now, viewed through the modern
perception of the president's home as a magnificent
castle, an American Buckingham Palace, remote,
mysterious, myth-bound, viewed distantly through
wrought-iron railings and, to almost every citizen,

inaccessible except on a limited tour. But in the
early days the average citizen could just walk right
in and ask to see the president.

And it wasn't even white—it is constructed of
gray and red sandstone painted white (according
to whitehouse.gov, it takes 570 gallons of white
paint to cover the whole facade).

President George Washington commissioned
its building, holding a competition for the best
design for the home. After a deal with famous
French architect Pierre L'Enfant, who designed
the layout of Washington, D.C. (basing it loosely
on Paris), fell apart, Irishman James Hoban won,
patterning it after Leinster House in Ireland.

The first stone was laid in 1792, but since it took
eight years to build, Washington died before it
was completed, making him the only president to
never live in it. His successor, John Adams, moved
in before the end of his presidency in 1800. Third
president Thomas Jefferson gave the White House
its distinctive columns and classic Greek-styled
entrance, and the house evolved over time as
different presidents added features.

The White House was built by slaves, something
former first lady Michelle Obama brought to public
consciousness when she remarked how mindful
she was of that every day she woke up in it.

In the beginning it was commonly referred
to as "the President's House" and, somewhat
off-message, "the President's Palace," but more

Washington, D.C., features similar roundabouts as its model, Paris.

DID YOU KNOW?

Many exotic animals have lived in the White House, including an alligator, a bobcat, a wallaby, and both lion and bear cubs.

The last major renovation on the building was done under Harry Truman and completed in 1952.

The White House, then called the President's House, was ready for its first first family in 1800.

READY FOR ITS CLOSE-UP

Below: The very first photo of the White House—a view of the south facade in 1846.

officially as "the Executive Mansion." President Teddy Roosevelt rechristened it the White House, to give it a sort of solid dignity and make a distinction between the president's and state governors' residences, which were also known as executive mansions.

In 1812, the Americans were back to fighting the British, who burned down most of Washington as they claimed the city in 1814, including the White House. Hoban was brought in once again to rebuild it, which took three years. Most of the original structure was destroyed, but a new version was erected on the foundation.

James Monroe added the South Portico in 1824; five years later Andrew Jackson built the North Portico. Theodore Roosevelt moved the offices from the residence portion of the White House to the newly constructed Executive Office building, which we know today as the West Wing. But it was William Howard Taft who built the iconic Oval Office where the president does much of the daily business of running the country.

The White House has swelled to a current 55,000 square feet, with 132 rooms, 35 bathrooms and 412 doors—but surprisingly, many fewer windows; there are only 147 of them, and none of them open! There are 28 fireplaces and, for those keeping count, eight staircases versus only three elevators. The president's residence occupies six levels. The house and grounds cover 18 acres. There's been a bowling alley there since Harry Truman wanted one. John F. Kennedy converted the space into an indoor swimming pool that he used every day as therapy for his chronic back problems. (He also apparently used it for midday trysts.) The subsequently moved bowling alley was made into a basketball court by Barack Obama, and Kennedy's now-unused pool lies beneath the Press Briefing Room.

The modern White House is one of the grandest and most luxurious places to live on the planet— few homes have their own chocolate kitchen, flower shop, bowling alley, 42-seat cinema and dentist's office.

It's one of the most haunted, too, with one set of characters who benignly hover around the halls. Harry Truman, who described the White House as a "glamorous prison," was convinced he was not alone, writing to his wife who was away one night about hearing a loud knocking on the bedroom door: "I jumped up and put on my bathrobe, opened the door, and no one was there. Went out and looked up and down the hall, looked in your room and Margie's. Still no one. Went back to bed after locking the doors and there were footsteps in your room whose door I'd left open. Jumped and looked and no one there! The damned place is haunted sure as shootin'. Secret Service said not even a watchman was up here at that hour. You and Margie had better come back and protect me before some of these ghosts carry me off."

The British army burned the White House in 1814 during the War of 1812.

Abraham Lincoln's ghost has been seen the most often, and it's said he appears "when the country needs him most," walking up and down the corridors. Winston Churchill saw him, saying that as he got out of a bath, he looked up and Lincoln was standing there. The naked Churchill quipped, "You have me at a disadvantage, Mr. President." First lady Grace Coolidge told of seeing Lincoln in his old office, looking out the window. Dutch Queen Wilhelmina found him sitting on her bed. And there was only one room that Ronald Reagan's dog was afraid to go into—the Lincoln Bedroom. And other spirits, including former Presidents Thomas Jefferson, William Henry Harrison, John Tyler and Andrew Jackson, are said to still be roaming the halls, legends that just won't leave.

ANDREW
JACKSON

TRYING TO APPEAL TO THE COMMON MAN,
JACKSON EXPANDED THE NATION BY FORCIBLY
RELOCATING NATIVE AMERICAN TRIBES

★ ★ ★

RANKING
14

ANDREW JACKSON, A MILITARY HERO WHOSE STAR ROSE when he led his army of volunteers to victory in the Battle of New Orleans in the War of 1812, was by all accounts quick-tempered, strong-willed, fearless and "tough as old hickory wood," earning him the nickname "Old Hickory."

Jackson was easily elected to office in 1828, four years after the "Corrupt Bargain," when the House of Representatives chose John Quincy Adams as president over Jackson, who'd won the popular vote but failed to achieve a majority in the Electoral College (see page 37). Jackson became known for being the first Democratic president after he and his supporters founded the Democratic Party, a few years after Jefferson and Madison's Democratic-Republican party faded away.

Still annoyed by the 1824 election debacle, he made numerous failed pleas to Congress to abolish the Electoral College. He also booted out incumbent officeholders and replaced them with his supporters in a move that is now known as the "spoils system."

The Tennessean cast himself as the People's President—"the people are the sovereigns; they

KEY ACHIEVEMENTS

• Erased the national debt, freeing the United States of foreign and domestic obligations beyond the reserves of the Treasury.

• Negotiated a trade agreement with Great Britain that opened the U.S. to trade with Canada and the British West Indies.

• Limited the powers of banks, putting financial liberty in the hands of the people.

can alter and amend," and in his inaugural address, promised a restrained federal government, the protection of states' rights and fair treatment of Native Americans. That latter promise became a controversial one that Jackson did not live by, leading some historians to wonder if the former slave owner should be revered or reviled.

In an article from 1958 titled "Andrew Jackson Versus the Historians" in the *Journal of American History*, author Charles Grier Sellers Jr. points out that in 1856, James Parton, one of the first biographers of Jackson, called him "a patriot and traitor."

At the time of his election, the nation was flush with the possibility of expansion. Looking to open up land for the settlement of U.S. citizens and recognizing that Western lands were cheap for speculators (he speculated himself, grabbing and developing about 45,000 acres in the Tennessee River Valley), Jackson convinced Congress to adopt the Removal Act in 1830, whereby land west of the Mississippi River would be granted to native tribes if they agreed to give up

DID YOU KNOW?

Jackson's 1829 Inauguration Day turned into a mob scene as large crowds pressed through the White House, seeking out the populist president to congratulate him.

Jackson survived the first attempted presidential assassination when both of his attacker's guns misfired.

their homelands. By signing this document into law, Jackson became the first U.S. president to create a systematic approach to the federal removal of Indian tribes. Since, legally, tribes acknowledged themselves "to be under the protection of the United States of America, and of no other sovereign whosoever," Jackson was able to build a case whereby the president could provide lands out West, often typically offering government assistance to native Americans in relocating. In his message to Congress in December 1830, Jackson called his expansionist efforts "but a continuation of the same progressive change by milder process."

While a few tribes went peacefully, including the Chickasaws, the Choctaws, the Creeks and the Seminoles, all of whom signed treaties that required them to uproot to the far side of the Mississippi River, the Cherokee Nation of Georgia held out. When the Supreme Court ruled that they were sovereign and immune from Georgia's laws, President Jackson ignored their ruling and obtained a signature from a minority Cherokee chief in the Treaty of Echota in 1835.

1829–1837

BORN MARCH 15, 1767, WAXHAWS, SOUTH CAROLINA
DIED JUNE 8, 1845, NASHVILLE, TENNESSEE
BURIAL SITE THE HERMITAGE, NASHVILLE, TENNESSEE
EDUCATION NO FORMAL DEGREES
POLITICAL PARTY DEMOCRATIC
AGE AT INAUGURATION 61
VICE PRESIDENTS JOHN C. CALHOUN (1ST TERM); MARTIN VAN BUREN (2ND TERM)
OPPONENTS JOHN QUINCY ADAMS (1ST TERM); HENRY CLAY, JOHN FLOYD, WILLIAM WIRT (2ND TERM)
OCCUPATIONS BEFORE PRESIDENCY LAWYER, SOLDIER, POLITICIAN
OTHER OFFICES ATTORNEY GENERAL OF WESTERN DISTRICT OF NORTH CAROLINA; DELEGATE TO TENNESSEE STATE CONSTITUTIONAL CONVENTION; U.S. CONGRESSMAN; U.S. SENATOR; TENNESSEE SUPREME COURT JUDGE; GOVERNOR OF FLORIDA TERRITORY
FIRST LADY RACHEL DONELSON ROBARDS JACKSON
NICKNAME OLD HICKORY

DID YOU KNOW?
Jackson's opponents called him a "jackass" for his populist views. Entertained by this insult, Jackson used the image of the donkey for the symbol of the Democratic Party.

BLOODY SUNDAY
Jackson leads his motley crew of an army during the Battle of New Orleans in 1815.

Today, historians agree that Jackson's aggressive westward vision of settlement and profitable real estate opportunities could only have succeeded through the subjugation of native tribes. By the end of his presidency, he had signed into law nearly 70 removal treaties, paving the way for the settlement of Western territories. The remaining Cherokee Nation members who tried to hold onto their land were forcibly removed during a brutal march westward in 1836, known as the Trail of Tears. Roughly 20,000 Cherokees were forced to move, with about a quarter perishing along the way.

"I TRY TO LIVE MY LIFE AS IF DEATH MIGHT COME FOR ME AT ANY MOMENT."

ANDREW JACKSON

MARTIN
VAN BUREN

THE DEMOCRATIC ARCHITECT BUILT HIS PARTY,
BUT FROZE IN THE FACE OF ECONOMIC CRISIS

★ ★ ☆

RANKING
22

NICKNAMED THE LITTLE MAGICIAN FOR BOTH HIS SLEIGHTY political craft and petite frame, the 5-foot-6 Martin Van Buren began his political career blueprinting party appointments, and by the time he earned a U.S. Senate seat in 1821, he found himself presiding over a sophisticated state organization he himself had engineered.

He was a "transforming political figure in American history," wrote Joel Silbey in *Martin Van Buren and the Emergence of American Popular Politics*, "a persistent and innovative practitioner of a new style of national politics." But that new style may not have been all that effective.

Upon entry to the White House, Van Buren, the first president to be born a citizen of the United States, continued his closed-door work as a party craftsman, paying little attention to looming national concerns. Met with the mammoth financial crisis of the Panic of 1837 just two months into his presidency, an unprepared Van Buren refused to allow the government to intervene as a massive bank failure set in motion an economic

KEY ACHIEVEMENTS

• Resolved tensions along the border between Maine and New Brunswick, Canada, which was under British control.

• Opposed the Patriot War—raids by unauthorized militias on Canada—which helped improve relations between the U.S. and Canada.

free fall the nation had never before seen. The resulting break in the American West speculative real estate market created a domino effect on the U.S. economy, upending product prices, profits and wages and leaving nearly a quarter of the population in some regions unemployed.

Desperate to strengthen the nation, Van Buren sought to expand territory by furthering the brutal Native American relocation programs, initially designed by his mentor and predecessor, Andrew Jackson. An expensive and shameful conflict with the Seminole tribes in Florida—the Seminole people fought upwards of 5,000 American troops sent to the area and thousands perished—damaged both his public and interparty standing. It ultimately cost Van Buren reelection in 1840, losing to William Henry Harrison and the Whig party, who believed the forced removal campaign was inhumane. In 1844 Van Buren ran again, but still under the specter of his first term, failed to gain the Democratic nomination.

DID YOU KNOW?
Born to Dutch parents who emigrated to the United States, Van Buren is the only president whose second language was English.

1837–1841

BORN DEC. 5, 1782, KINDERHOOK, NEW YORK
DIED JULY 24, 1862, KINDERHOOK, NEW YORK
BURIAL SITE KINDERHOOK CEMETERY, KINDERHOOK, NEW YORK
EDUCATION NO FORMAL DEGREES
POLITICAL PARTY DEMOCRATIC
AGE AT INAUGURATION 54
VICE PRESIDENT RICHARD M. JOHNSON
OPPONENT WILLIAM HENRY HARRISON
OCCUPATIONS BEFORE PRESIDENCY LAWYER, POLITICIAN
OTHER OFFICES SURROGATE OF COLUMBIA COUNTY, NEW YORK; NEW YORK STATE SENATOR; ATTORNEY GENERAL OF NEW YORK; DELEGATE TO THE THIRD NEW YORK STATE CONSTITUTIONAL CONVENTION; U.S. SENATOR; GOVERNOR OF NEW YORK; SECRETARY OF STATE; U.S. VICE PRESIDENT
FIRST LADY HANNAH HOES VAN BUREN
NICKNAMES LITTLE MAGICIAN, RED FOX OF KINDERHOOK, MARTIN VAN RUIN

Van Buren tried twice to win back the presidency but failed both times.

WILLIAM HENRY
HARRISON

HE INVENTED MODERN CAMPAIGNING AND WON IN A LANDSLIDE, BUT DIED SOON AFTER TAKING OFFICE

★ ★ ☆

RANKING
N/A

WILLIAM HENRY HARRISON HOLDS THE RECORD FOR shortest U.S. presidency (31 days) and was the first to die in office. Another wealthy Virginian from a political family, Harrison's father, Benjamin, had signed the Declaration of Independence. He joined the army at 18 and fought in the Northwest Indian War that resulted in the Native Americans ceding territory to the federal government and opening up a large swath of Ohio for settlement.

With his sterling military background, Harrison earned a leading post in the government of the Northwest Territory, which led him to Congress and then an appointment as Governor of Illinois for several terms. At the outbreak of the War of 1812, he resumed his military career as Commander of the Army of the Northwest, and led U.S. troops to victory against the British in several battles. His most important victory came in the Battle of the Thames, in which Shawnee leader Tecumseh—whom Harrison had fought against in the 1811 Battle of Tippecanoe to quash Indian rebellions against U.S. expansion—was killed. At the war's end in 1814, Harrison became a key figure in negotiating peace and land treaties with the Indians.

He remained in politics and although he lost to Martin Van Buren in 1836, Harrison's bid succeeded in the next election, as he slyly promoted himself as a humble frontiersman running against the wealthy, elitist Van Buren. Harrison's party, the Whigs, hailed his military career with the campaign slogan "Tippecanoe and Tyler, Too," referring to Harrison's running mate John Tyler, which helped usher him into office in a landslide victory.

Perhaps eager to show he was still the powerful leader of yesteryear, he rode on horseback in the cold rain to his inauguration on March 4, 1841, and then delivered a 105-minute, 8,445-word speech (the longest inaugural address in history) sans coat, hat or gloves. He then attended three inaugural balls.

Three weeks later, Harrison came down with a cold that only got worse. White House physicians treated him with experimental medicines and bloodletting, most of which weakened him further, and he died nine days later. Harrison's physician, Thomas Miller, said it was "pneumonia of the lower lobe of the right lung, complicated by congestion

"I CONTEND THAT THE STRONGEST OF ALL GOVERNMENTS IS THAT WHICH IS MOST FREE."

WILLIAM HENRY HARRISON

DID YOU KNOW?

Harrison is the only president who studied to become a doctor—and he was the last president to be born as a British subject.

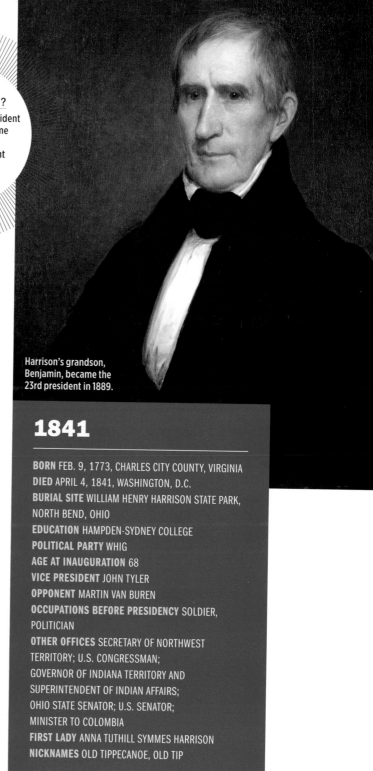

Harrison's grandson, Benjamin, became the 23rd president in 1889.

of the liver." But new evidence suggests otherwise. In 2014, *The New York Times* reported a modern-day medical investigation into Harrison's death revealed his primary illness may have been typhoid fever, which he may have contracted through the White House's contaminated water system.

On his deathbed, Harrison whispered to his vice president, "I wish you to understand the true principles of the government. I wish them carried out. I ask nothing more."

Despite his short time in office, Harrison is credited with transforming presidential elections. As biographer Gail Collins explains, his "Log Cabin and Hard Cider" campaign was the first to feature mass rallies, appearance by the candidate and catchy slogans like "Tippecanoe and Tyler, Too."

Collins describes Harrison's story as one that is "less about issues than about the accidents of fate and silly campaigns," claiming that even if Harrison had lived, the country would still have marched into the Civil War. "There was nothing in Harrison's history that suggests transformational leader."

Though little more than a footnote, Harrison's one-month term did raise the unexplored question of whether a standing vice president should formally assume the title and salary of a president upon the latter's passing, or simply execute the duties of presidential office. To answer, Vice President Tyler quickly presented a constitutional mandate granting himself the presidency upon completion of the presidential oath of office, establishing a future precedent for an orderly transfer of executive power.

1841

BORN FEB. 9, 1773, CHARLES CITY COUNTY, VIRGINIA
DIED APRIL 4, 1841, WASHINGTON, D.C.
BURIAL SITE WILLIAM HENRY HARRISON STATE PARK, NORTH BEND, OHIO
EDUCATION HAMPDEN-SYDNEY COLLEGE
POLITICAL PARTY WHIG
AGE AT INAUGURATION 68
VICE PRESIDENT JOHN TYLER
OPPONENT MARTIN VAN BUREN
OCCUPATIONS BEFORE PRESIDENCY SOLDIER, POLITICIAN
OTHER OFFICES SECRETARY OF NORTHWEST TERRITORY; U.S. CONGRESSMAN; GOVERNOR OF INDIANA TERRITORY AND SUPERINTENDENT OF INDIAN AFFAIRS; OHIO STATE SENATOR; U.S. SENATOR; MINISTER TO COLOMBIA
FIRST LADY ANNA TUTHILL SYMMES HARRISON
NICKNAMES OLD TIPPECANOE, OLD TIP

JOHN
TYLER

THE FIRST "ACCIDENTAL PRESIDENT," HE ESTABLISHED THE TRANSFER-OF-OFFICE PROCESS

★ ★ ★

RANKING
36

NICKNAMED "HIS ACCIDENCY," JOHN TYLER WAS THE first president involved in an incidental acquisition of office, and the self-defined process by which he, the elected vice president, assumed the presidency after William Henry Harrison died established the standard for future death-in-office procedures. But the transition was a challenging one for Tyler. Every member of his Cabinet except for his secretary of state resigned five months into his term.

In *John Tyler, The Accidental President*, author Edward P. Crapol admits Tyler, who was born into wealth and privilege and was an avid proponent for states' rights, was a "tragic figure" with an obscure presidency. Crapol acknowledges that Tyler was not a great president, but believes he was a "stronger and more effective president than generally remembered."

Still, Tyler had a lasting impact. After Harrison's passing from pneumonia,

KEY ACHIEVEMENTS

• Treaty of Wanghia opened trade in the Far East.

• Expanded Western territories by giving settlers the right to claim land before it was for sale and then buy it later for $1.25 an acre.

• Signed a tariff bill to protect Northern manufacturers.

President Tyler made strides to expand the Western territories with 1841's Preemption Act, a policy that offered 160 acres of affordable land for purchase to any American citizen. There's the Webster-Ashburton Treaty of 1842 that settled the U.S.-Canada border dispute with Great Britain, mainly along the Maine-Brunswick border and around the Great Lakes region, following the "bloodless" Aroostook War that took place from 1838 to 1839. Allegedly there were no casualties, but one legend has it that either a Canadian cow or pig wandering over the border was shot by mistake. Tyler further shaped American borders via the annexation of Texas, as well as an 1845 bill declaring Florida the 27th state.

On the global front, Tyler also secured the signing of 1884's Treaty of Wanghia, an agreement with China that granted American usage of Asian ports, opening the Far East for U.S. traders.

A year after assuming office, there was a measure in the House of Representatives to impeach Tyler for misuse of veto power.

DID YOU KNOW?
With his two wives, Tyler fathered 15 children (eight with his first wife; seven with his second). Two of his grandchildren were still alive in 2020.

1841–1845

BORN MARCH 29, 1790, CHARLES CITY COUNTY, VIRGINIA

DIED JAN. 18, 1862, RICHMOND, VIRGINIA

BURIAL SITE HOLLYWOOD CEMETERY, RICHMOND, VIRGINIA

EDUCATION COLLEGE OF WILLIAM AND MARY

POLITICAL PARTY WHIG

AGE AT INAUGURATION 51

VICE PRESIDENT NONE

OPPONENT NONE

OCCUPATION BEFORE PRESIDENCY LAWYER

OTHER OFFICES MEMBER OF VIRGINIA HOUSE OF DELEGATES; U.S. CONGRESSMAN; GOVERNOR OF VIRGINIA; U.S. SENATOR; U.S. VICE PRESIDENT

FIRST LADIES LETITIA CHRISTIAN TYLER, JULIA GARDINER TYLER

NICKNAMES ACCIDENTAL PRESIDENT, HIS ACCIDENCY

JAMES KNOX
POLK

DETERMINED TO EXPAND THE NATION,
HE FOCUSED ON CONNECTING THE COASTS

★ ★ ☆

RANKING
17

BOASTING GRAND AMBITIONS, JAMES POLK WAS A VIRTUAL unknown outside of political circles. He "lacked charisma, had no oratorical power, and no personal magnetism," said historian Robert Johannsen. "He was forbearing, modest, even dull." Yet he charmed a public hungry for new territory, yielding a hair's breadth victory over Henry Clay, the nationally known Whig candidate.

Polk's first two pledges, to expand the U.S. both north to Oregon and west to California, grew America's territory by more than a third while accomplishing the first cross-continental expansion. His third campaign promise, to reduce tariffs, materialized in the form of the 1846 Walker Tariff Act, a dual benefit that boosted trade with Britain while increasing U.S. market size. His final promise, the elimination of private holdings of federal funds, occurred one week after the Walker Act via the establishment of the first U.S. Treasury, a safeguard over the type of national financial implosion that marred Van Buren's administration.

KEY ACHIEVEMENTS

• Signed Buchanan-Pakenham Treaty with Great Britain, which set the northern boundary of the Oregon Territory.

• Created the Department of the Interior.

• Signed the Treaty of Guadalupe Hidalgo, ending the Mexican War, with Mexico agreeing to the southern boundary of Texas at the Rio Grande River and to cede California and New Mexico territories to the U.S.

Not all Polk-era expansion came without conflict, as the establishment of Northwest territories required the Mexican-American War. The conflict had kicked off in 1836 when Congress offered Texas annexation after its declaration of independence from Mexico. In 1845, after Texas officially became the 28th state of the Union, the newly elected Polk offered Mexico $20 million for the remainder of the present-day Southwest. Mexico refused, Polk declared war, and two years later a reduced $15 million payment was issued, extending the United States from the Atlantic to Pacific Ocean. Overall, Polk increased the size of the United States by 1.2 million square miles in just one term, the greatest territorial expansion of any president.

Over his four years, Polk displayed an efficiency that is yet to be replicated in the presidential office— "a legacy of leadership," says Johannsen, that Americans will surely come to appreciate.

DID YOU KNOW?
Polk held "office hours" two days a week, allowing the public to come visit him in the White House.

1845–1849

BORN NOV. 2, 1795, MECKLENBURG COUNTY, NORTH CAROLINA

DIED JUNE 15, 1849, NASHVILLE, TENNESSEE

BURIAL SITE STATE CAPITOL GROUNDS, NASHVILLE, TENNESSEE

EDUCATION UNIVERSITY OF NORTH CAROLINA

POLITICAL PARTY DEMOCRATIC

AGE AT INAUGURATION 49

VICE PRESIDENT GEORGE M. DALLAS

OPPONENT HENRY CLAY

OCCUPATION BEFORE PRESIDENCY LAWYER

OTHER OFFICES MEMBER OF TENNESSEE LEGISLATURE; U.S. CONGRESSMAN; SPEAKER OF THE HOUSE OF REPRESENTATIVES; GOVERNOR OF TENNESSEE

FIRST LADY SARAH CHILDRESS POLK

NICKNAMES YOUNG HICKORY, NAPOLEON OF THE STUMP

Polk died at home, just a few months after leaving office.

ZACHARY
TAYLOR

TABBED "OLD ROUGH AND READY" ON THE BATTLEFIELD,
TAYLOR LACKED POLITICAL KNOW-HOW IN OFFICE

★ ★ ☆

RANKING
34

A NATIONALLY RECOGNIZED WAR HERO AT THE TIME OF HIS election, Major General Zachary Taylor was the first president to be elected without having held any prior political office. A descendant of powerful Southern plantation owners, Taylor's 40 years of army service included commanding positions in the War of 1812, the Black Hawk War, 1835's second Seminole War and a high-profile role in the Mexican-American War that earned him the nickname "Old Rough and Ready."

After the last battle, despite his general disinterest in politics—"The idea that I should become President... has never entered my head, nor is it likely to enter the head of any other person"—the Whig Party flattered Taylor into joining the presidential ticket alongside vice presidential candidate Millard Fillmore.

A thin Whig victory slid the pair into the White House, where hotly contested proposals to expand slavery were leading to threats of Southern secession. Though a slaveholder himself, the enigmatic Taylor held preservation of the Union

KEY ACHIEVEMENT

• Signed Clayton-Bulwer Treaty with Britain to expand U.S. commercial interests and build a Central American canal.

above all other goals and refused to support extension of slavery into the newly established Western territories and Mexican Cession. To avoid alienating constituents, Taylor instead encouraged settlers in New Mexico and California to draw their own constitutions for statehood, bypassing territorial establishment, which allowed them to determine their own laws.

In the summer of 1850, just 16 months into his term, Taylor suddenly fell ill after drinking milk and eating cherries during an extremely hot July 4 ceremony and died of gastroenteritis (some experts say it may have actually been a form of cholera) before achieving any substantial advancement regarding the status of slavery.

Taylor's presidency didn't fail so much as it has been forgotten. According to Jay Tolson in *U.S. News & World Report*, he "was probably the least politically attuned man to occupy the White House in American history, ignorant, one might say, to the point of innocence."

DID YOU KNOW?

Taylor was a second cousin of the fourth president, James Madison.

1849–1850

BORN NOV. 24, 1784, ORANGE COUNTY, VIRGINIA

DIED JULY 9, 1850, WASHINGTON, D.C.

BURIAL SITE JEFFERSON COUNTY, KENTUCKY

EDUCATION NO FORMAL DEGREES

POLITICAL PARTY WHIG

AGE AT INAUGURATION 64

VICE PRESIDENT MILLARD FILLMORE

OPPONENT LEWIS CASS

OCCUPATIONS BEFORE PRESIDENCY SOLDIER, FARMER

OTHER OFFICES NONE

FIRST LADY MARGARET "PEGGY" MACKALL SMITH TAYLOR

NICKNAME OLD ROUGH AND READY

A career military officer, Taylor never voted for a presidential candidate before his election.

MILLARD
FILLMORE

A BLAND TERM MADE FILLMORE AN OFFICIAL SYNONYM FOR MEDIOCRITY

★ ★ ☆ —————————————————————————

RANKING
37

AS A DISILLUSIONED VICE PRESIDENT UNDER ZACHARY Taylor, Millard Fillmore was granted little input, relegated to moderating heated Congressional debates regarding slavery and serving mainly as a calming agent when voices got too loud.

But when a mistreated stomach sickness took the life of President Taylor in July 1850, Fillmore was drawn out of the din and into the spotlight. Though a personal opponent of slavery—"God knows I detest slavery, but it is an existing evil"—Fillmore upheld the principles of his predecessor's hard-line Union preservation agenda. The resulting Compromise of 1850—a complex agreement led by Whig Senator Henry Clay and Democratic Senator Stephen Douglas—ended the slave trade in Washington, D.C., but aided Southern efforts to recover fugitive slaves, gave New Mexico and Utah territories the right to determine their own slavery policies, and granted California entrance into the Union as a free state.

KEY ACHIEVEMENTS

- Treaty of Kanagawa in 1854 with the Japanese allowed U.S. to trade in two Japanese ports.

- Supported the Compromise of 1850, averting the Civil War for another 11 years.

- Refused to invade Cuba to create a slave colony.

- Protected the Hawaiian islands from being taken over by France.

Fillmore's ongoing enforcement of the Compromise of 1850's Fugitive Slave Act drew heavy criticism from his former supporters in the North, and in 1852 the Whig Party chose to pass him over for reelection.

Fillmore did manage to overcome an 1851 blaze that threatened to incinerate the Library of Congress, destroying two-thirds of the Library's collection of 55,000 volumes. A professed bibliophile known to carry a dictionary everywhere he went, Fillmore signed a bill to replace all burnt books and paid personally to establish the first White House library.

Millard Fillmore: Biography of a President author Robert J. Rayback notes the 13th president was "not a clever politician or an inspiring orator"—even the White House's official presidential directory describes him as "uninspiring"—but "more importantly if promotion and preservation of the nation are the criteria, he was a statesman with only a handful of White House rivals," writes Rayback.

DID YOU KNOW?

Fillmore was one of the original founders of the University of New York at Buffalo. He was chancellor from 1846 to 1874.

1850–1853

BORN JAN. 7, 1800, LOCKE, CAYUGA COUNTY, NEW YORK

DIED MARCH 8, 1874, BUFFALO, NEW YORK

BURIAL SITE FOREST LAWN CEMETERY, BUFFALO, NEW YORK

EDUCATION NO FORMAL DEGREES

POLITICAL PARTY WHIG

AGE AT INAUGURATION 50

VICE PRESIDENT NONE

OPPONENT NONE

OCCUPATIONS BEFORE PRESIDENCY APPRENTICE TO CLOTH DRESSER, APPRENTICE TO WOOL CARDER, LAWYER

OTHER OFFICES MEMBER OF NEW YORK LEGISLATURE; U.S. CONGRESSMAN; U.S. VICE PRESIDENT

FIRST LADY ABIGAIL POWERS FILLMORE

NICKNAME THE AMERICAN LOUIS PHILIPPE

Born in a log cabin in upstate New York, Fillmore spent much of his

FRANKLIN
PIERCE

YOUNG PIERCE'S MORAL INDECISION LED TO NATIONAL RUPTURE

★ ★ ★

RANKING
38

APPROACHING THE ELECTION OF 1852, THE U.S. FOUND itself enjoying a state of real economic strength and superficial social repose. The Compromise of 1850 had soothed regional conflicts regarding slavery policies in new American territories, though tempers were left broiling and building beneath the surface. After announcing his full support for the bill, 47-year-old Democratic presidential candidate Franklin Pierce privately pledged loyalty to New England backers and Southern delegates alike.

Pierce was involved in a train crash two months prior to his inauguration in which his 11-year-old son Benjamin was killed, but he got down to work upon his election. He immediately promoted settlement in new Northwestern territories, upsetting abolitionists who found his push beneficial to those looking to take slavery into unregulated lands. Concurrently, Pierce's Southern supporters fed his impatience with abolitionists by arguing that new Northwestern railroads could further strengthen the economy. Pierce sought to appease both sides by endorsing the Kansas–Nebraska Act of 1854, a bill that was supposed "to organize the Territory of Nebraska," an area covering the present-day states of Kansas, Nebraska, Montana and the Dakotas. It made slavery in these new territories a decision of popular sovereignty over congressional dictate, essentially repealing 1820's Missouri Compromise.

The following spring, pro-slavery Missourians flooded Kansas intent on electing sympathetic lawmakers and triggering massive conflicts with incoming abolitionists. Violence soon entered the halls of democracy itself, as a fistfight between Southern and abolitionist senators erupted on the U.S. Senate floor. Pierce, loyal to neither side, refused to send federal troops to halt the Kansas chaos, leading embarrassed Democrats to deny him reelection in 1856.

Pierce is considered this country's most obscure president, having a murky and difficult presidency during a very unstable period for the nation. Upon his death, *The New York Herald* wrote the "deceased was a man of something more than average ability. He possessed, however, none of the attributes of greatness, and was more of a cautious, studious and watchful politician than a comprehensive, far-seeing or observant statesman."

KEY ACHIEVEMENTS

• Signed Kansas-Nebraska Act allowing the people in those two territories to decide for themselves whether to allow slavery within their borders.

• U.S. bought land from Mexico that later became part of Arizona and New Mexico as part of the Gadsden Purchase.

DID YOU KNOW?
Pierce was elected to the
New Hampshire State
Legislature at the age
of 24; within two years he
was elected its Speaker
of the House.

Pierce joined
the temperance
movement when he
married, but began
drinking heavily near
the end of his life.

1853–1857

BORN NOV. 23, 1804, HILLSBORO,
NEW HAMPSHIRE
DIED OCT. 8, 1869, CONCORD, NEW HAMPSHIRE
BURIAL SITE OLD NORTH CEMETERY, CONCORD,
NEW HAMPSHIRE
EDUCATION BOWDOIN COLLEGE
POLITICAL PARTY DEMOCRATIC
AGE AT INAUGURATION 48
VICE PRESIDENT WILLIAM R. KING
OPPONENT WINFIELD SCOTT
OCCUPATIONS BEFORE PRESIDENCY LAWYER,
POLITICIAN, SOLDIER
OTHER OFFICES SPEAKER OF NEW HAMPSHIRE
LEGISLATURE; U.S. CONGRESSMAN; U.S. SENATOR;
PRESIDENT OF NEW HAMPSHIRE CONSTITUTIONAL
CONVENTION
FIRST LADY JANE MEANS APPLETON PIERCE
NICKNAMES YOUNG HICKORY OF THE GRANITE HILLS,
HANDSOME FRANK

JAMES
BUCHANAN

*INEPT AND CORRUPT, BUCHANAN WATCHED
THE NATION IMPLODE INTO WAR*

★ ★ ★

**RANKING
41**

NEARLY UNANIMOUSLY CONSIDERED BY HISTORIANS TO BE THE worst president ever—for being indecisive and inactive (historian Samuel Morison called him a president who "prayed and frittered and did nothing")—James Buchanan entered office as a Democrat professing opposition to slavery while defending the disastrous Kansas–Nebraska Act of 1854 and the Lecompton Constitution, a failed attempt to legalize slavery in Kansas. On occasion, Buchanan tried to appease both sides by suggesting one dime was a fair daily wage for manual labor, earning him the nickname "Ten-Cent Jimmy." He continued to habitually pass the buck and pivot, shrugging the following year that slavery was a territory and states' rights issue protected by the U.S. Constitution, rather than a severe moral violation all presidents were obligated to prevent.

Buchanan's utter lack of character proved itself during his pre-inaugural interference with the legendary Dred Scott Supreme Court case, wherein—in seeking to make a pro-slavery decision more palatable to Northerners—he privately and illegally convinced Pennsylvania native Justice Robert Cooper Grier to vote with a Southern stance. Grier obliged, voting to deny the federal government the right to ban slavery, while supporting the concept that no African Americans could be afforded basic citizenship and legal rights and, effectually, none of the human dignities of its white citizens.

The Dred Scott decision benefited no one, as new territories soon became full-on theaters of battle that prefaced the impending war. As complete national fracture began, Buchanan watched seven Southern states secede from the Union, declaring himself anti-secession while refusing to provide any of the order his bleeding nation needed. The 1860 election saw Abraham Lincoln succeed a staggered Buchanan. One month later, after the secession of South Carolina and the formation of the Confederacy, the bloody Civil War began.

"WHATEVER THE RESULT MAY BE, I SHALL CARRY TO MY GRAVE THE CONSCIOUSNESS THAT I AT LEAST MEANT WELL FOR MY COUNTRY." JAMES BUCHANAN

1857–1861

BORN APRIL 23, 1791, COVE GAP, PENNSYLVANIA
DIED JUNE 1, 1868, LANCASTER, PENNSYLVANIA
BURIAL SITE WOODWARD HILL CEMETERY, LANCASTER, PENNSYLVANIA
EDUCATION DICKINSON COLLEGE
POLITICAL PARTY DEMOCRATIC
AGE AT INAUGURATION 65
VICE PRESIDENT JOHN C. BRECKENRIDGE
OPPONENT JOHN C. FREMONT
OCCUPATION BEFORE PRESIDENCY LAWYER
OTHER OFFICES MEMBER OF PENNSYLVANIA LEGISLATURE; U.S. CONGRESSMAN; MINISTER TO RUSSIA; U.S. SENATOR; SECRETARY OF STATE; MINISTER TO GREAT BRITAIN
FIRST LADY BUCHANAN NEVER MARRIED; HARRIET REBECCA LANE JOHNSTON, HIS NIECE, ACTED AS "HOSTESS" FOR HER UNCLE
NICKNAMES TEN-CENT JIMMY, OLD BUCK

DID YOU KNOW?
Buchanan is the only president to remain a lifelong bachelor.

Some experts today speculate Buchanan may have suffered from exodeviation, or a wandering eye.

SECOND IN
COMMAND

*THE VICE PRESIDENT IS NOT AS GLAMOROUS
OF A ROLE AS ONE MIGHT THINK*

★ ★ ★

OVER THE YEARS, THE WAY THAT U.S. VICE PRESIDENTS have been appointed or elected has varied, but they have almost always ducked the limelight in favor of letting the president be front and center.

Early in the nation's history, the presidential candidate who was the runner-up in electoral votes became the vice president. In 1800, Thomas Jefferson and Aaron Burr tied for the presidency, so the House of Representatives was left to decide. As a result, the 12th Amendment to the Constitution was adopted in 1804, mandating that the president and vice president run together. Jefferson later chose George Clinton, the governor of New York, to run with him on the same ticket.

Clinton did such a good job as a quiet No. 2 man that he also served as veep under James Madison. (John C. Calhoun is the only other vice president to have served in two administrations, for John Quincy Adams and Andrew Jackson.)

Still, some vice presidents became well-known over time. Eight of them (John Tyler, Millard Fillmore, Andrew Johnson, Chester A. Arthur, Theodore Roosevelt, Calvin Coolidge, Harry S. Truman and Lyndon B. Johnson) became president after the commander in chief died in office; one (Gerald Ford) took the title after a president's resignation.

The 25th Amendment, ratified on February 10, 1967, allows the vice president to serve as acting president, just temporarily, if the president is ill or temporarily unable to fulfill their Constitutional duties. George H.W. Bush did just this, serving as acting president for eight hours while President Ronald Reagan had a cancerous polyp in his large intestine removed on July 13, 1985. And Ford became the first vice president selected under the 25th Amendment after Spiro Agnew resigned. When Ford became president after Richard Nixon's resignation, he appointed Nelson Rockefeller to be his No. 2.

Rockefeller was an active and occasionally blunt leader. The JFK Library quotes him as telling his aides, "I'm not interested in what I can't do. I want

Franklin D. Roosevelt's choice of Truman as a running mate for his fourth term had history-making consequences.

Throughout Ronald Reagan's two terms as president, George H.W. Bush was his loyal No. 2.

WHO'S NEXT?

THE LINE OF SUCCESSION TO BECOME PRESIDENT IS LONG

Per Article 2, Section 1, Clause 6 of the Constitution, if the president can no longer serve—he's removed from office, dies, resigns or has the inability to discharge the "Power and Duties of the Office"—the vice president serves. But what if he's unable to? Who then takes over? To whom do we turn for leadership?

If the vice president cannot serve, next in line is the speaker of the House, then the Senate president pro tempore, then Cabinet members, in this order:

1 Secretary of State
2 Secretary of the Treasury
3 Secretary of Defense
4 Attorney General
5 Secretary of the Interior
6 Secretary of Agriculture
7 Secretary of Commerce
8 Secretary of Labor
9 Secretary of Health and Human Services
10 Secretary of Housing and Urban Development
11 Secretary of Transportation
12 Secretary of Energy
13 Secretary of Education
14 Secretary of Veterans Affairs
15 Secretary of Homeland Security

Also, in the case of a national emergency or disaster, like the COVID-19 pandemic, the sitting president cannot cancel or postpone a general election by executive order. And under the U.S. Constitution, a president and vice president cannot stay in office past their four-year terms without being reelected. So, if a general election does not occur, for any reason, the Constitution's rules and order of succession automatically kick in.

to know how I can do what I want to do and it is your job to tell me." He was considered one of the more moderate or liberal Republicans, inspiring the phrase "Rockefeller Republicans," and had an interest in supporting the environment, arts and education. But the office held its limits, and he decided not to run again with Ford in 1976.

Once in office, those who were second in command found it easier to stay in power: Teddy Roosevelt, Coolidge, Truman and Lyndon Johnson were eventually reelected after finishing a predecessor's term.

Still, many veeps have stewed that their time serving in office was largely one of frustration. John Nance Garner, who was VP for two terms under Franklin Delano Roosevelt, famously declared that "the vice presidency is not worth a bucket of warm spit."

While many veeps have been content to stay in the background, some of have taken a more active role. Journalist and historian Jules Witcover, who wrote *The American Vice Presidency: From Irrelevance to Power*, said in an interview in *Smithsonian* magazine that Dick Cheney was one of the most "influential and involved" vice presidents while serving under George W. Bush, but his "influence in war-making and expanding presidential powers also [was] the most controversial." Cheney helped determine policy for the "war on terror" in Iraq and Afghanistan and was criticized for Bush administration policies including the CIA's use of torture when interrogating terrorism suspects. He has been quoted as saying, "It is easy to take liberty for granted when you've never had it taken from you."

But Witcover also noted that even in recent history, vice presidents have mostly taken a back seat: "With only two Constitutional functions, to replace the president in the event of death, disability or resignation and to preside over the Senate, they had no governing duties in the executive branch, and in fact were considered part of the legislative branch for purposes of salary. Presidents were uninclined or unwilling to delegate governing roles to them, and the office was not often sought after."

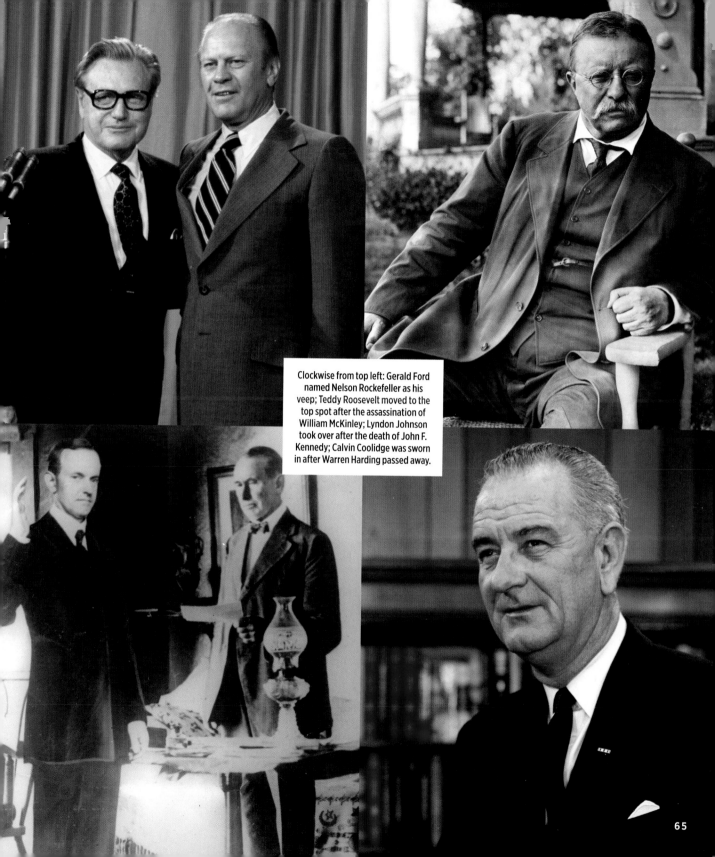

Clockwise from top left: Gerald Ford named Nelson Rockefeller as his veep; Teddy Roosevelt moved to the top spot after the assassination of William McKinley; Lyndon Johnson took over after the death of John F. Kennedy; Calvin Coolidge was sworn in after Warren Harding passed away.

ABRAHAM
LINCOLN

NO MATTER HOW TURBULENT THE TIMES WERE, LINCOLN LED THE NATION THROUGH ITS DARKEST POLITICAL CRISIS

★ ★ ★

RANKING
1

BORN IN A ONE-ROOM LOG CABIN IN RURAL KENTUCKY, our tallest president (towering at 6 feet 4 inches), Abraham Lincoln, wasn't fond of recalling details of his early life, telling one biographer, "It can all be condensed into a single sentence and that sentence you will find in Gray's 'Elegy'—'The short and simple annals of the poor.'" This serious, poor and humble man grew up to be the most revered (and most studied) president in American history. And his presidency was one that was consumed by the Civil War, the worst war ever fought on U.S. soil.

Lincoln—boatman, postmaster, store clerk, shopkeeper and, most famously, a self-taught lawyer— entered local politics in 1834, associating himself with the Whig Party, whose members opposed President Andrew Jackson and the Democrats. The Whigs fell into disarray over the issue of slavery in the 1850s. The nail in the Whig coffin was the passage of the Kansas-Nebraska Act in 1854: Authored by Illinois Senator Stephen Douglas, the bill mandated "popular sovereignty," allowing each territory to permit slavery within its borders. Lincoln abhorred the notion and was compelled to speak out against it—and most Whig Party members, including Lincoln, switched to Republican membership over the issue.

A captivating orator who was able to draw sizable crowds, Lincoln catapulted to national attention as he engaged in a legendary series of debates against Douglas across Illinois in the 1858 election for U.S. Senate. Lincoln eloquently opposed slavery while simultaneously avoiding a radical position that would alienate moderate voters.

His campaign opened on a prophetic note, declaring, "A house divided against itself cannot stand." Fundamental to his argument was a conviction that slavery itself was morally wrong and ran counter to the wishes of the Founding Fathers.

Lincoln lost the Senate election but gained national acclaim, going on to win the Republican Party nomination in 1860. He captured less than 40 percent of the popular vote but secured a majority in the Electoral College with the votes of the free states alone. His win immediately triggered the secession of 11 Southern states from the Union and was the catalyst for the Civil War.

KEY ACHIEVEMENTS

• Signed the Homestead Act that allowed any citizen (even if impoverished) to obtain land.

• Established the Department of Agriculture.

• Issued the Emancipation Proclamation, leading to the abolishment of slavery.

DID YOU KNOW?
Lincoln grew a beard after an 11-year-old child wrote to him, saying it would appeal to more voters.

Lincoln only had about 18 months of formal schooling in his life.

Lincoln visits Major General John A. McClernand (right) at Antietam, Maryland. At left is Allan Pinkerton, head of Lincoln's security detail.

DID YOU KNOW?
Lincoln genuinely hated being called Abe, preferring Abraham or Lincoln.

Although a vocal opponent of the expansion of slavery into new territories, he was not an abolitionist, holding firm the belief that the Constitution prevented the outright abolishment of slavery in states where it already existed. His view was laid plain in his 1861 inaugural address: "I have no purpose, directly or indirectly, to interfere with the institution of slavery in the states where it exists. I believe I have no lawful right to do so, and I have no inclination to do so."

Slavery was a deeply divisive political hot button, since the Founding Fathers never explicitly differentiated between "person" and "property" in the Constitution. The moral implications of slavery were intensely debated. Moreover, historians are quick to assert that the issue of slavery was not solely a moral fight but

1861–1865

BORN FEB. 12, 1809, HARDIN COUNTY, KENTUCKY
DIED APRIL 15, 1865, WASHINGTON, D.C.
BURIAL SITE OAK RIDGE CEMETERY, SPRINGFIELD, ILLINOIS
EDUCATION NO FORMAL DEGREES
POLITICAL PARTY REPUBLICAN
AGE AT INAUGURATION 52
VICE PRESIDENTS HANNIBAL HAMLIN (1ST TERM); ANDREW JOHNSON (2ND TERM)
OPPONENTS JOHN C. BRECKENRIDGE, STEPHEN DOUGLAS (1ST TERM); GEORGE McCLELLAN (2ND TERM)
OCCUPATIONS BEFORE PRESIDENCY STORE CLERK, STORE OWNER, FERRY PILOT, SURVEYOR, POSTMASTER, LAWYER
OTHER OFFICES MEMBER OF ILLINOIS GENERAL ASSEMBLY; U.S. CONGRESSMAN
FIRST LADY MARY TODD LINCOLN
NICKNAMES ABE, HONEST ABE, ILLINOIS RAIL-SPLITTER

DOLLAR, DOLLAR BILL, Y'ALL!

You have to be a colossal figure in U.S. history to get your mug on its currency. Besides the usual suspects gracing the $1, $5, $10, $20, $50 and $100 bills, and even that hard-to-find $2 bill with Thomas Jefferson, there are also several denominations that are no longer produced: $500 (William McKinley), $1,000 (Grover Cleveland), $5,000 (James Madison), $10,000 (Salmon P. Chase—the sixth chief justice of the Supreme Court) and the $100,000 note (Woodrow Wilson).

Jefferson, along with George Washington and Lincoln, are the only presidents to grace currency that both folds and jingles, while Alexander Hamilton and Benjamin Franklin are the only non-presidents to have their portraits on money.

During the birth of our nation, coins featured symbols such as Lady Liberty and the American eagle on the back. But by 1909, in order to mark the 100th anniversary of Lincoln's birth, the Franklin Mint issued a new commemorative penny with the 16th president's face.

A little over two decades later, a commemorative coin was issued for Washington. The Washington quarter remains in production today. In 1938, the Treasury Department held a $1,000 competition to solicit a new image for the five-cent coin, and Jefferson replaced the Buffalo nickel, also known as the Indian Head nickel.

Soon after World War II and the death of Franklin Roosevelt, his role as founder of The March of Dimes made his portrait the perfect fit to adorn the 10-cent piece. And following the assassination of President John F. Kennedy, his bust replaced Franklin on the half-dollar.

As we move toward the inclusion of more women who have helped shape our country on currency, current and past honorees include Native American guide Sacagawea, suffragist Susan B. Anthony, advocate for the deaf and blind Helen Keller, and several first ladies. And Martha Washington is featured on more than just a coin—she's the only woman to have been on paper currency, having appeared on silver certificates in the late 19th century.

"NEARLY ALL MEN CAN STAND ADVERSITY, BUT IF YOU WANT TO TEST A MAN'S CHARACTER, GIVE HIM POWER." ABRAHAM LINCOLN

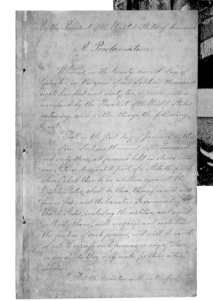

an economic one, since the defenders of slavery in the South argued that their economy was dependent on slave labor and that it was a natural state of humankind. In their book *A Just and Generous Nation: Abraham Lincoln and the Fight for American Opportunity*, authors Harold Holzer and Norton Garfinkle suggest that "more than is often realized, the Civil War was fought not over the morality of slavery or the abstract sanctity of the American Union, but over what kind of economy the nation should have."

Unrest, division, turmoil and war marked the first year of Lincoln's presidency. From December 1860 through June 1861, the 11 states that severed ties with the Union arranged a provisional government adopting a new name, the Confederate States of America. Throughout this first year, Lincoln remained adamant that this withdrawal of Southern states was in direct violation

This is a page from Lincoln's Emancipation Proclamation, delivered January 1, 1863.

of the Constitution and he was to use any means necessary to hold onto the "world's last best hope": American democracy.

The Confederates attacked Fort Sumter, South Carolina, on April 12, 1861, to start the war, and Lincoln announced a naval blockade to Southern ports, engaging the cooperation of foreign countries in recognizing the Southern states as belligerent in the Civil War.

On January 1, 1863, Lincoln began the new year with his Emancipation Proclamation, freeing almost 20,000 slaves in states that had seceded

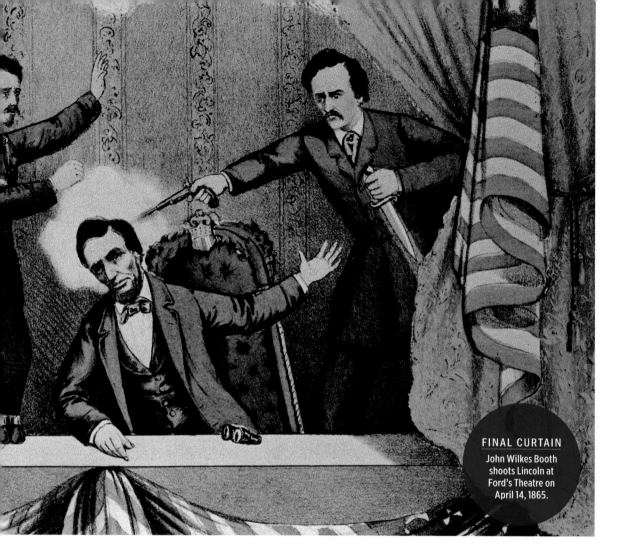

FINAL CURTAIN

John Wilkes Booth shoots Lincoln at Ford's Theatre on April 14, 1865.

from the Union. This executive order established the freedom of slaves as a war goal and proved to be a morale boost for the Union. For years, Lincoln spoke and argued against slavery. "What do you do with slavery, given that it's unjust?" asked historian Eric Foner. "Lincoln took a very long time to try to figure out exactly what steps ought to be taken."

Campaigning on a constitutional amendment to end slavery, Lincoln was elected to a second term amidst the raging conflict. By the time he was sworn in, the war was drawing to a close and Lincoln's tone in his inaugural address was one of peace, with a conciliatory outlook on postwar Reconstruction. In January 1865—just

months before Confederate General Robert E. Lee surrendered to Union General Ulysses S. Grant—the 13th Amendment, making slavery unconstitutional, was ratified and became law.

Only weeks into his second term, Lincoln's presidency and his Reconstruction efforts were cut short on April 14, 1865, when he was shot at Ford's Theatre in Washington, D.C., by Confederate sympathizer John Wilkes Booth. Lincoln died the following morning, just six days after the surrender of General Lee. He remains forever embedded in the consciousness of American history as our country's greatest leader during our darkest moral and political crisis.

ANDREW JOHNSON

JOHNSON'S POOR MORALS LED TO THE NATION'S FIRST IMPEACHMENT

★ ★ ★

RANKING
40

PROPELLED BY HIS ORATORICAL SKILLS, ANDREW JOHNSON, who had to follow in Abraham Lincoln's very large footsteps after his assassination, began the first years of Reconstruction sparring with Republicans in Congress over his support of rebel states electing ex-Confederate officials who wanted to pass laws that were designed to repress freed slaves.

Born and raised in the South and having come to national politics after holding local offices in Tennessee, Johnson firmly believed the U.S. Constitution protected the "American right" of slave ownership. After assuming office, he vetoed the Freedmen's Bureau Act—designed to provide aid to the formerly enslaved—in 1866. (The House and Senate were able to override the veto to pass the act.) And despite Congressional passage of the 14th Amendment, Johnson continued to urge the Southern states to fight ratification of black citizenship.

Mounting hostilities between Johnson (a Democrat who'd run with Lincoln during the Civil War on a special "National Union" ticket) and the Republican Congress came to a head in early 1868 when the House leveled impeachment charges for his violation of the Tenure of Office Act after his unexplained removal of Secretary of War Edwin Stanton, who was a staunch opponent of the president's pro-slavery stance. Johnson was impeached by Congress but acquitted of any crime by the Senate. Having tired of his public spats and antiquated stances, the Democratic party chose not to endorse Johnson for re-election the following year.

Johnson believed in Lincoln's policies and was a symbol of loyalty to Washington. But in his book *Andrew Johnson: A Biography*, Hans L. Trefousse ponders: "How was it that a statesman who experienced a spectacular rise from homeless newcomer to Governor and Senator, a political leader who succeeded in routing not only the powerful organizers of the opposing party but also the numerous antagonists in his own, a general who ruled with an iron hand as military governor in Tennessee, could be so seemingly inept in carrying out the functions of the office of President of the United States?"

KEY ACHIEVEMENTS

• Outlined a Reconstruction plan for North Carolina that became the blueprint for other Southern states.

• Bought Alaska from Russia for $7.2 million in gold.

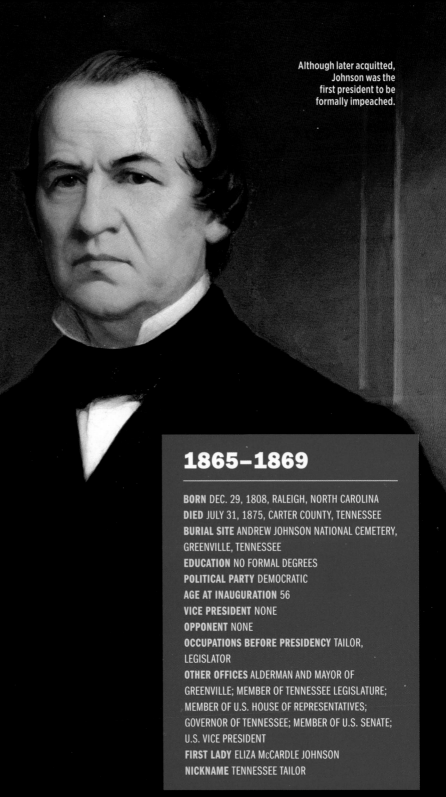

Although later acquitted, Johnson was the first president to be formally impeached.

DID YOU KNOW?

Johnson served in the Senate following his departure from office, the only president ever to do so following his presidential term.

1865–1869

BORN DEC. 29, 1808, RALEIGH, NORTH CAROLINA
DIED JULY 31, 1875, CARTER COUNTY, TENNESSEE
BURIAL SITE ANDREW JOHNSON NATIONAL CEMETERY, GREENVILLE, TENNESSEE
EDUCATION NO FORMAL DEGREES
POLITICAL PARTY DEMOCRATIC
AGE AT INAUGURATION 56
VICE PRESIDENT NONE
OPPONENT NONE
OCCUPATIONS BEFORE PRESIDENCY TAILOR, LEGISLATOR
OTHER OFFICES ALDERMAN AND MAYOR OF GREENVILLE; MEMBER OF TENNESSEE LEGISLATURE; MEMBER OF U.S. HOUSE OF REPRESENTATIVES; GOVERNOR OF TENNESSEE; MEMBER OF U.S. SENATE; U.S. VICE PRESIDENT
FIRST LADY ELIZA McCARDLE JOHNSON
NICKNAME TENNESSEE TAILOR

ULYSSES S. GRANT

THE CIVIL WAR HERO FOUGHT AS PRESIDENT TO BRING EQUALITY TO FORMER SLAVES

★ ★ ★

RANKING
27

ONE WEEK BEFORE ULYSSES S. GRANT, THE COUNTRY'S first four-star general since George Washington, took office, Congress proposed the 15th Amendment, stating that the right to vote could not be denied "on account of race, color or previous condition of servitude."

In his inaugural address, Grant stated that the issue of suffrage was "likely to agitate the public" until settled. "I entertain the hope and express the desire," he declared, that its settlement "may be by ratification of the 15th...amendment." Grant worked steadfastly to assure the ratification of the amendment and on February 3, 1870, it was signed into law, giving black men the right to vote.

This issue of suffrage and the larger policy of Reconstruction of the United States following the Civil War was a heated one. Grant's predecessor, Andrew Johnson, emulated the vision of Abraham Lincoln and promoted the forgiveness of the South, with the hope of unifying the country as swiftly as possible.

KEY ACHIEVEMENTS

- Established Yellowstone National Park, the country's first national park.

- Oversaw completion of the Transcontinental Railroad.

- Signed the Civil Rights Act of 1875, guaranteeing black Americans equal rights in public places and prohibiting their exclusion from jury duty.

Johnson's policies gave the white South agency to negotiate the transition of free blacks without measures in place to secure their new rights. In turn, freed blacks were denied any roles in governance.

Cited as our nation's first terrorist group, the Tennessee-born Ku Klux Klan, originally a social club for Confederate veterans, began to give rise to anti-black and Radical Republican sentiments, violence and murder. Grant responded with a pitch to Congress urgently recommending "such legislation as in the judgment of Congress shall effectually secure life, liberty, and property and the enforcement of law in all parts of the United States." Congress followed with The Enforcement Acts, three bills passed between 1870 and 1871 that were criminal codes that protected the rights of black Americans to vote, to hold office, to serve on juries and to receive equal protection of laws.

In the most violent of counties in South Carolina, Grant suspended the writ of

DID YOU KNOW?

At age 46, Grant was the youngest president at that point in U.S. history. (The youngest ever was Theodore Roosevelt, who was 42 in 1901 when he assumed the office.)

While a successful military officer, Grant failed in several business enterprises.

Known for his aggressive battlefield style, he earned the nickname "Unconditional Surrender" Grant.

"THE ART OF WAR IS SIMPLE ENOUGH. FIND OUT WHERE YOUR ENEMY IS. GET AT HIM AS SOON AS YOU CAN. STRIKE HIM AS HARD AS YOU CAN, AND KEEP MOVING ON." ULYSSES S. GRANT

habeas corpus to ensure that any Klansman arrested could not be released from captivity by sympathizers. In Grant's post-Civil War administration, his policies on Reconstruction were firmly grounded in the notion that the spirit of the old ways of the South and the planters' mentality must die if there was to be equal protection of blacks and whites under the law.

Despite being a leader on the battlefield, history professor Joan Waugh says as a two-term president, Grant "is typically dismissed as weak and ineffective." But Waugh says the quiet and soft-spoken Grant has been reevaluated by historians for possessing a "coherent political philosophy." She points out that Grant oversaw a "powerful if unstable" economy, which was a result of the war, and presided over the completion of the Transcontinental Railroad from Sacramento, California to Omaha, Nebraska, just two months after his inauguration in 1869. Grant did win

reelection in 1872, in the largest popular-majority victory for a Republican in the 19th century —55.6 percent—but his second term was marred by controversy, including impeachment articles brought against Secretary of War William W. Belknap for accepting bribes.

Still, Grant gets tremendous praise for fighting for both African-American and Native American rights and civil service reform, as well as execution of an effective foreign policy. He opted not to run for a third term, choosing retirement instead.

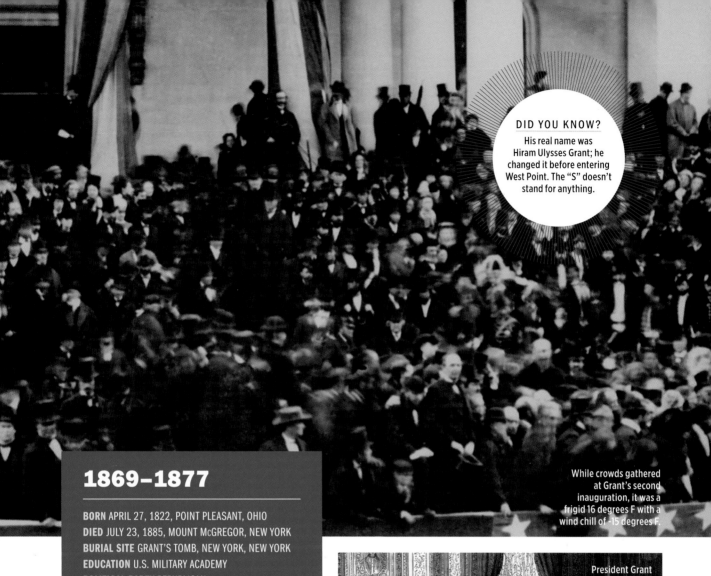

DID YOU KNOW?
His real name was
Hiram Ulysses Grant; he
changed it before entering
West Point. The "S" doesn't
stand for anything.

While crowds gathered
at Grant's second
inauguration, it was a
frigid 16 degrees F with a
wind chill of -15 degrees F.

1869–1877

BORN APRIL 27, 1822, POINT PLEASANT, OHIO
DIED JULY 23, 1885, MOUNT McGREGOR, NEW YORK
BURIAL SITE GRANT'S TOMB, NEW YORK, NEW YORK
EDUCATION U.S. MILITARY ACADEMY
POLITICAL PARTY REPUBLICAN
AGE AT INAUGURATION 46
VICE PRESIDENTS SCHUYLER COLFAX (1ST TERM);
HENRY WILSON (2ND TERM)
OPPONENTS HORATIO SEYMOUR (1ST TERM);
HORACE GREELEY (2ND TERM)
OCCUPATIONS BEFORE PRESIDENCY SOLDIER;
FARMER; REAL ESTATE AGENT; CUSTOM HOUSE CLERK;
LEATHER STORE CLERK
OTHER OFFICES NONE
FIRST LADY JULIA BOGGS DENT GRANT
NICKNAMES HERO OF THE APPOMATTOX;
"UNCONDITIONAL SURRENDER" GRANT

President Grant
signed an
anti-Ku Klux Klan
bill into law
in 1871.

RUTHERFORD B.
HAYES

SUPPOSEDLY ENDING RECONSTRUCTION,
HAYES MAY HAVE DONE THE EXACT OPPOSITE

★ ★ ★

RANKING
29

RUTHERFORD B. HAYES WAS ENJOYING RETIREMENT— he was a lawyer, Civil War veteran and former governor of Ohio—when his fellow Republicans called upon him to unretire in order to run against New York Democratic Governor Samuel Tilden in the 1876 presidential election. Tilden won by 250,000 more popular votes. However, a constitutional crisis ensued when competing sets of electoral returns from Florida, Louisiana, South Carolina and Oregon remained unresolved.

At the request of then-President Ulysses S. Grant, an electoral commission was formed and Hayes was handed the presidency in a secret meeting between Republican representatives and Southern Democrats. With this informal deal, known as The Compromise of 1877, Republicans promised that Hayes would remove troops from the South in exchange for their support. Additional agreed-upon points that were not documented included the appointment of a Southern Democrat to the president's Cabinet, legislation to help industrialize the South and mend its economy, and the right of the South to handle the civil liberties of blacks without federal interference.

KEY ACHIEVEMENTS

- Appropriated funds for internal improvements in the South.

- Forbade the involvement of federal employees in political activities to curtail corruption.

- Supported a canal uniting the Atlantic and Pacific Oceans, leading to the building of the Panama Canal.

Hayes inherited a Democratic Congress and a Supreme Court that eviscerated protections set forth in the 14th Amendment (and later in the Civil Rights Act of 1883). This so-called Reconstruction Amendment, ratified in 1868, granted citizenship to "all persons born or naturalized in the United States," including former and recently freed slaves. It also forbade states from denying any person "life, liberty or property, without due process of law" or to "deny to any person within its jurisdiction the equal protection of the laws." But maintaining the involvement of federal troops to protect the civil liberties of blacks was implausible in this political climate.

Thomas J. Culbertson, director emeritus of the Rutherford B. Hayes Presidential Center, acknowledges that "from around 1900 through the 1950s, Hayes was praised as the man who reunited the nation and ended that awful period known as Reconstruction"—and the removal of federal troops from Louisiana and South Carolina is often cited as the end of that era. But journalist Nikole Hannah-Jones sees things differently. She wrote

DID YOU KNOW?

Hayes was the first president to have a telephone and a typewriter in the White House.

Hayes' wife, Lucy, was the first president's wife to have graduated from college.

1877–1881

BORN OCT. 4, 1822, DELAWARE, OHIO

DIED JAN. 17, 1893, FREMONT, OHIO

BURIAL SITE SPIEGEL GROVE STATE PARK, FREMONT, OHIO

EDUCATION KENYON COLLEGE, HARVARD LAW SCHOOL

POLITICAL PARTY REPUBLICAN

AGE AT INAUGURATION 54

VICE PRESIDENT WILLIAM A. WHEELER

OPPONENT SAMUEL J. TILDEN

OCCUPATION BEFORE PRESIDENCY LAWYER

OTHER OFFICES MEMBER OF U.S. HOUSE OF REPRESENTATIVES; GOVERNOR OF OHIO

FIRST LADY LUCY WARE WEBB HAYES

NICKNAMES DARK-HORSE PRESIDENT, HIS FRAUDULENCY, RUTHERFRAUD

in *The New York Times*, "With the troops gone, white Southerners quickly went about eradicating the gains of Reconstruction," calling the period between the 1880s and 1930s a "second slavery."

A more modern lens tells us that the backdoor deal that sealed Hayes' presidency also assured the rise of Southern white supremacy and ushered in an era of Jim Crow laws that demoralized Southern blacks. Hayes did not seek reelection and he spent his final years dedicating himself to work in public education and prison reform.

JAMES
GARFIELD

GARFIELD'S BRIEF BUT RESPECTABLE TERM HELPED RESTORE PRESIDENTIAL INTEGRITY

★ ★ ★

RANKING
N/A

JAMES A. GARFIELD HOLDS THE DISTINCTION OF BEING THE last president born in a log cabin. Raised on an Ohio farm by his impoverished mother following the death of his father when Garfield was just 2, the boy wanted to be a sailor and dreamed of travel. After spending nine terms in the House of Representatives, he was headed for his biggest adventure when he won the presidency, albeit barely—he led the popular election by less than 10,000 votes.

Garfield, who'd served as a colonel in the Union Army during the Civil War and was subsequently elected to Congress, identified as a Radical Republican who sought a firm plan of Reconstruction for the South and believed education would be the key to improving the lives of African Americans.

But upon entering the White House, Garfield was met with a deluge of political appointment requests from both traditionalist and progressives, all hungry to restore the party to their liking. Determined to favor merit over affiliation, Garfield took four months to set his cabinet. His frustration in the process was clear when he said, "My day is frittered away by personal seeking of people, when it ought to be given to the great problem[s] which concern the whole country."

KEY ACHIEVEMENTS

• Strengthened Federal authority over the New York Customs House.

• Supported education for black Southerners and called for African American suffrage.

Finally, he identified his first presidential mission as civil service reform, for which he became a "martyred symbol," according to historian Carter Smith. That's because less than one month later, on July 2, 1881, Charles Julius Guiteau—a resentful lawyer whom Garfield had denied appointment—shot the president in the back as he walked through the Washington train station on his way to a family vacation. Guiteau surrendered but pronounced himself a "Stalwart" (aka conservative) Republican. "[Chester A.] Arthur is now president of the United States."

That statement wasn't initially true. The president survived the assassination attempt—for a while—and inventor Alexander Graham Bell attempted to locate the bullet using a primitive type of metal detector, but he was unsuccessful. On September 19, 1881, with the bullet still lodged in his back, Garfield succumbed to his wounds. (Guiteau was hanged on June 30, 1882, just two days before the first anniversary of his shooting of the president.)

Garfield, a man of great intention but little accomplishment, only served in office for 199 days—the second-shortest presidential term, behind William Henry Harrison's one-month stint.

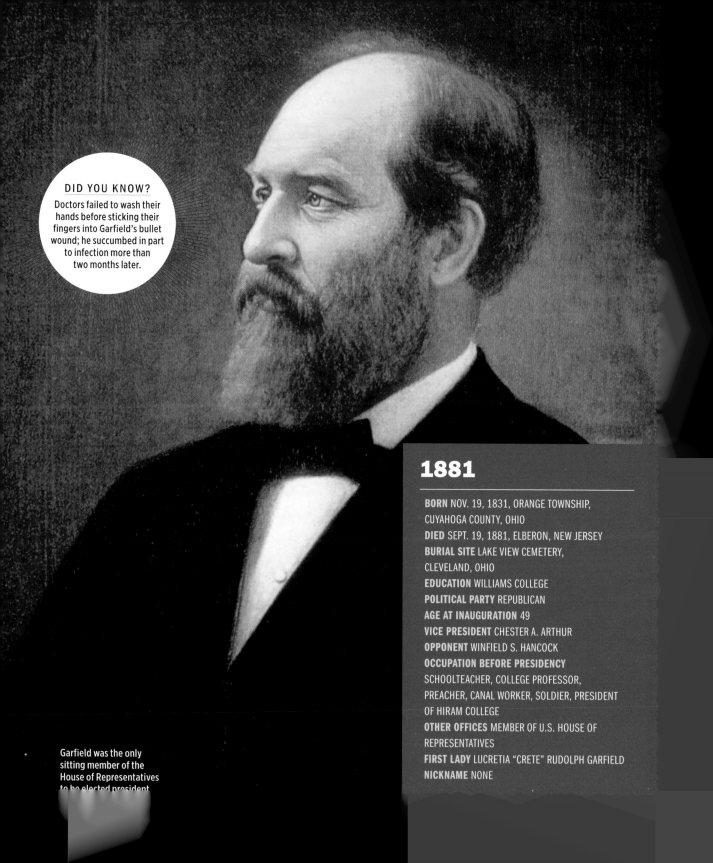

DID YOU KNOW?
Doctors failed to wash their hands before sticking their fingers into Garfield's bullet wound; he succumbed in part to infection more than two months later.

1881

BORN NOV. 19, 1831, ORANGE TOWNSHIP, CUYAHOGA COUNTY, OHIO
DIED SEPT. 19, 1881, ELBERON, NEW JERSEY
BURIAL SITE LAKE VIEW CEMETERY, CLEVELAND, OHIO
EDUCATION WILLIAMS COLLEGE
POLITICAL PARTY REPUBLICAN
AGE AT INAUGURATION 49
VICE PRESIDENT CHESTER A. ARTHUR
OPPONENT WINFIELD S. HANCOCK
OCCUPATION BEFORE PRESIDENCY SCHOOLTEACHER, COLLEGE PROFESSOR, PREACHER, CANAL WORKER, SOLDIER, PRESIDENT OF HIRAM COLLEGE
OTHER OFFICES MEMBER OF U.S. HOUSE OF REPRESENTATIVES
FIRST LADY LUCRETIA "CRETE" RUDOLPH GARFIELD
NICKNAME NONE

Garfield was the only sitting member of the House of Representatives to be elected president.

CHESTER A.
ARTHUR

NOT MUCH WAS EXPECTED FROM ARTHUR, SO HE REBUILT
THE HIGHEST OFFICE IN THE LAND, LITERALLY

★ ★ ☆

RANKING
31

WHEN YOU'RE A U.S. PRESIDENT DESCRIBED AS ONE WHO "frequently lands on lists of the country's most obscure chief executives," as Scott S. Greenberger wrote in *The Unexpected President: The Life and Times of Chester A. Arthur*, not much is expected of you.

Arthur's political career was propelled by New York Republican machinery and he spent those years publicly tearing down the system, becoming "a strong and effective president, a courageous anti-corruption reformer, and an early civil rights advocate," wrote Greenberger.

Born in Vermont and the son of a Baptist preacher, during a brief New York law career Arthur was co-opted by city Republican boss Roscoe Conkling, who slid the young attorney his first real "political" job with the city's Port Authority. Conkling and the machine took a particular liking to Arthur, and ensured a swift carriage up the Republican rungs to vice president. After the assassination of James Garfield, President Arthur entered office, and he began the process of trying to switch off the political machines.

In 1883, Arthur displayed a baffling change of heart in signing the Pendleton Act, a law designed to wrench the gears of the spoils system, wherein parties blanket their boosters, friends and family members—qualifications aside—with employment. Then he assembled a bipartisan Civil Service Commission just to enforce the act, ensuring government jobs were only awarded to those who deserved them.

Arthur, known as the "Father of the Steel Navy," rebuilt the United States Navy, ordering the production of steel cruisers, steel rams and steel gunboats at a time when the military branch was nearly forgotten.

Always well-dressed (it's rumored he owned 80 pairs of trousers), Arthur's Reconstruction efforts included actual reconstruction. He refurbished the White House, which he described as "badly kept barracks," with famed designer and Tiffany glass namesake Louis Comfort Tiffany. The pet project cost Congress $30,000 (approximately $2 million in today's value) and discarded 20 wagonloads of old furnishings, while ignoring the ever-increasing federal budget surplus. Unfortunately, Arthur wasn't able to enjoy this new elegance. Suffering from what would be a fatal kidney disease, he did not seek reelection in 1884.

KEY ACHIEVEMENTS

• Signed the Pendleton Act, ensuring government jobs for qualified applicants.

• Helped spark the modernization of the U.S. Navy.

DID YOU KNOW?
It's a long-standing rumor that Arthur was actually born in Canada, not Vermont.

1881–1885

BORN OCT. 5, 1830, NORTH FAIRFIELD, VERMONT
DIED NOV. 18, 1886, NEW YORK, NEW YORK
BURIAL SITE RURAL CEMETERY, ALBANY, NEW YORK
EDUCATION UNION COLLEGE
POLITICAL PARTY REPUBLICAN
AGE AT INAUGURATION 50
VICE PRESIDENT NONE
OPPONENT NONE
OCCUPATIONS BEFORE PRESIDENCY TEACHER, SCHOOL PRINCIPAL, LAWYER
OTHER OFFICES QUARTERMASTER GENERAL OF NEW YORK STATE; NEW YORK COLLECTOR OF CUSTOMS
FIRST LADY ELLEN LEWIS HERNDON ARTHUR
NICKNAMES THE GENTLEMAN BOSS, ELEGANT ARTHUR

As a widower in the White House, Arthur asked his sister, Mary McElroy, to assume first lady duties.

STEPHEN GROVER
CLEVELAND

*THE HEAVY-HANDED BUT WELL-INTENTIONED REFORMER SACKED
CORRUPTION BUT STALLED IN THE FACE OF SOCIETAL UPROAR*

★ ★ ☆

RANKING
21

DURING HIS CLIMB FROM LOCAL TO NATIONAL POLITICS,
New York Democrat Grover Cleveland's
overarching agenda was to dismantle every corrupt
political machine he encountered.
The results reverberated well beyond
top political realms, slowing purely
partisan job appointments of all
types and infuriating Democrat
voting bases across the nation. And
as the only president to serve two
nonconsecutive terms, Cleveland
both optimistically reconstructed
and painfully experienced the
eventual results of his honest efforts.

Upon initial election, Cleveland,
who "tried so hard to do right," made
swift and fierce use of his veto powers
to battle "pork politics"—federal
spending that catered purely to special interests.
During his first 60 days in office he shot down eight
bills from the legislature; by the end of his second
term, he had invoked a veto on 414 occasions—a
record that stood until Franklin Roosevelt sunk
635 bills (albeit over his 12 years in office).

Cleveland's second term proved him a
dangerously slow thinker. The Panic of 1893 found
him stalled as a credit crisis, a stock market crash,
bank failures and multiple railroad shutdowns
rocked America. Labor strikes followed and
Cleveland panicked, sending
federal forces to end the stoppages.

On the issue of women's suffrage,
Cleveland was mostly silent,
believing this was a social problem
and that government should not
interfere with it. In an article for
Ladies' Home Journal, he wrote
that "man and woman have each
a separate and distinct, but an
equally important, place in the
world. Man has his work. Woman
has hers. But neither should invade
the other's province."

Cleveland left a tarnished legacy,
having accomplished electoral system repair but
no true national advancement, and despite being
in office two nonconsecutive terms, was ranked by
historians as an "average president at best." Upon
reflecting on his political career, he said, "I am
honest and sincere in my desire to do well, but the
question is whether I know enough to accomplish
what I desire."

**KEY
ACHIEVEMENTS**

• Vetoed hundreds of bills
as part of his belief in
limited government and
the ideals of the
U.S. Constitution.

• Modernized the
U.S. Navy and ordered
battleships that went on
to fight in the Spanish-
American War of 1898
and World War I.

DID YOU KNOW?
Grover Cleveland is the only sitting president to get married inside the White House.

Cleveland won his first presidential election by a margin of 1,200 votes in his home state of New York—just enough to bring him into office.

1885–89, 1893–97

BORN MARCH 18, 1837, CALDWELL, NEW JERSEY
DIED JUNE 24, 1908, PRINCETON, NEW JERSEY
BURIAL SITE PRINCETON, NEW JERSEY
EDUCATION NO FORMAL DEGREES
POLITICAL PARTY DEMOCRATIC
AGES AT INAUGURATION 47, 55
VICE PRESIDENTS THOMAS A. HENDRICKS (1ST TERM); ADLAI STEVENSON (2ND TERM)
OPPONENTS JAMES G. BAINE (1ST TERM); BENJAMIN HARRISON (2ND TERM)
OCCUPATIONS BEFORE PRESIDENCY CLERK, TEACHER, LAWYER
OTHER OFFICES ERIE COUNTY ASSISTANT DISTRICT ATTORNEY; SHERIFF OF ERIE COUNTY; MAYOR OF BUFFALO; GOVERNOR OF NEW YORK
FIRST LADY FRANCES FOLSOM CLEVELAND
NICKNAMES BIG STEVE, UNCLE JUMBO

BENJAMIN
HARRISON

*HIS HONEST EFFORTS TO PROTECT AND UNITE A RECOVERING
NATION LED IT TO THE BRINK OF ECONOMIC COLLAPSE*

★ ★ ☆

**RANKING
30**

FOLLOWING GROVER CLEVELAND'S SHAKEDOWN OF corrupt electoral machinery, William Henry Harrison's grandson, Republican Benjamin Harrison, set his sights on breaking conspiratorial big-business conglomerates. What followed was the Sherman Antitrust Act in 1890, a groundbreaking legislative move designed to increase economic competitiveness by prohibiting oppressive business practices, such as trade restraints and the formation of monopolies. Although the historic act yielded few immediate results, it did set the stage for Theodore Roosevelt's expansive antitrust sweep that took place just a decade later.

Unlike his predecessor's national rebuilding plan, Harrison's agenda included bold efforts to expand America's role in global affairs, though the well-intentioned attempts yielded mixed results. While Harrison did foster the first meeting of the future Pan-American Union, as well as founding a Samoan Island U.S. protectorate in league with Great Britain and Germany, he failed in his ongoing quest to annex Hawaii, as well as in gaining congressional support for the construction of a canal in Nicaragua.

On the domestic front, the former Civil War general fought for continued veterans' benefits, expanded the U.S. Navy, and as a passionate naturalist, endeavored to preserve American forests. His belief in equal rights for African Americans and Native Americans, however well-meaning, remained little more than a political stance, as he took thousands of acres of land away from American Indians.

Intending to enrich American businesses, Harrison elevated general tariffs near the end of his term. However, this action triggered rapid price increases for all consumers, resulting in the Panic of 1893. The imbalanced U.S. economic climate couldn't bear the sudden shift and a weary Harrison passed a nation that was teetering on the verge of financial ruin back to incoming second-term President Grover Cleveland.

KEY ACHIEVEMENTS

• Set precedent for America's democratic business climate.

• Stabilized life for veterans and widened the military.

• Positioned the U.S. as an international unifier.

DID YOU KNOW?
Harrison was the
first president to have
electricity in the
White House.

Harrison was the last
Civil War general to
serve as president.

1889–1893

BORN AUG. 20, 1833; NORTH BEND, OHIO
DIED MARCH 13, 1901; INDIANAPOLIS, INDIANA
BURIAL SITE CROWN HILL CEMETERY, INDIANAPOLIS,
INDIANA
EDUCATION MIAMI UNIVERSITY
POLITICAL PARTY REPUBLICAN
AGE AT INAUGURATION 55
VICE PRESIDENT LEVI P. MORTON
OPPONENTS GROVER CLEVELAND; CLINTON B. FISH
OCCUPATIONS BEFORE PRESIDENCY LAWYER,
NOTARY PUBLIC, SOLDIER
OTHER OFFICES COMMISSIONER FOR THE COURT
OF CLAIMS; CITY ATTORNEY; SECRETARY OF INDIANA
REPUBLICAN CENTRAL COMMITTEE; STATE SUPREME
COURT REPORTER; MEMBER OF U.S. SENATE
FIRST LADY CAROLINE SCOTT HARRISON
NICKNAMES KID GLOVES HARRISON, LITTLE BEN

WILLIAM
McKINLEY

*HIS DUAL APPROACH OF BUSINESS-BUILDING AND OVERSEAS
EXPANSION YIELDED NATIONAL PROSPERITY AND TRUST*

★ ★ ★

RANKING
19

POWERED BY THE OHIO POLITICAL MACHINE, FORMER Union Army Major William McKinley reached Congress just as his wartime commander, President Rutherford B. Hayes, entered the White House. Schooled by Hayes during his decade-plus as a Republican congressman, McKinley rose to chair of the House Ways and Means Committee, where he honed his signature Reconstruction-ready platform of economic protectionism. The Tariff Act of 1890 imparted steady increases on imported goods. Coupled with business-friendly domestic policies, it generated both high industrial profit and steady blue-collar work, soothing a populace still shaken from the depression of 1893.

His favor among big-business entities led Populist Democrat William Jennings Bryan, his presidential opponent in both 1896 and 1900, to attack McKinley as a puppet of industry monopolies. But Bryan's radical financial stances, including support of silver coinage as well as gold, proved too risky for a nation set on simply regaining its footing, and McKinley swept both races. Later in life he recalled, "I have never been in doubt since I was old enough to think intelligently that I would someday be made president."

KEY ACHIEVEMENTS

• The McKinley Tariff Act served both industry and labor.

• National prosperity repaired American pride after the depression of 1893.

• Bolstered U.S. presence in world affairs.

The president's boldest reconstructive moves occurred on foreign soil, where he expanded America's role in world affairs as well as its territorial holdings. In 1898, Spain's bloody repression of native Cuban revolutionaries, fed by the incidental explosion of the U.S. battleship *Maine* in Havana, which killed 266 soldiers (the origins of the explosion are still debated), resulted in the Spanish-American War, a swift conflict that gained Cuba its independence while earning America possession of Puerto Rico, Guam and the Philippines.

Next came the "Open Door Policy," opening the Chinese trade market to all nations and allowing the U.S. to stake crucial commercial interests in the region. The consequent Boxer Rebellion, a Chinese nationalist conflict which threatened the policy, was swiftly suppressed in a high-profile display of America's growing global power.

McKinley's second term came to an abrupt end when Leon Czolgosz, an unemployed anarchist, shot him twice in the chest; gangrene set in and he died eight days later, making him the third sitting president to be assassinated.

McKinley ran against and defeated the same opponent (William Jennings Bryan) in both his first and second terms.

DID YOU KNOW?
Mount McKinley in Alaska—a state the late president never stepped foot in—was renamed to Denali in 2015.

1897–1901

BORN JAN. 29, 1843, NILES, OHIO
DIED SEPT. 14, 1901, BUFFALO, NEW YORK
BURIAL SITE CANTON, OHIO
EDUCATION ALLEGHENY COLLEGE, ALBANY LAW SCHOOL
POLITICAL PARTY REPUBLICAN
AGE AT INAUGURATION 54
VICE PRESIDENTS GARRET A. HOBART; THEODORE ROOSEVELT
OPPONENT WILLIAM JENNINGS BRYAN
OCCUPATIONS BEFORE PRESIDENCY TEACHER, SOLDIER, LAWYER
OTHER OFFICES MEMBER OF U.S. HOUSE OF REPRESENTATIVES; GOVERNOR OF OHIO
FIRST LADY IDA SAXTON McKINLEY
NICKNAME IDOL OF OHIO

THEODORE
ROOSEVELT

THERE MAY NOT HAVE EVER BEEN A GREATER FORCE OF NATURE TO LEAD THIS COUNTRY — AND CERTAINLY THERE WAS NO GREATER FORCE FOR NATURE THAN ROOSEVELT

★ ★ ★

RANKING
5

A RAPID SOCIAL REFORMER WHO BROKE UP CORPORATE monopolies while bringing improved pay and conditions for the American workingman, Theodore Roosevelt was also a war hero whose dedication to military preparedness turned the United States into a global power. And he was a man so dedicated to the conservation of America's natural beauty that he turned millions of acres of unprotected wilderness into an expansive network of national parkland that remains without equal on the face of the Earth.

Vice President Roosevelt became the youngest commander in chief when he rose to the presidency at age 42 in March 1901 after President William McKinley was assassinated. The transition was agonizing for young Teddy, who had tirelessly campaigned for his mentor and predecessor, covering more than 21,000 miles to stump for him. But he took on the task with the kind of vigor that became his signature.

Roosevelt's youthful enthusiasm served him well from the start. He declared that America should be animated by "lofty ideals" that would speak not only to "the things of the body," but also to "the things of the soul."

KEY ACHIEVEMENTS

• Ensured the construction of the Panama Canal.

• Kept the door of China open to American commerce.

• Signed into legislation safety measures for food and medicine.

• Established national parks to protect millions of acres of wilderness.

The popular Roosevelt won reelection easily, trouncing Democratic candidate Alton Parker by nearly 200 electoral votes. In the first moments of his inaugural message to Congress in 1905, Roosevelt expressed a unique and innovative progressive domestic platform. He introduced his "Square Deal" domestic plan that promised he would go toe-to-toe with large industrial businesses that threatened to monopolize free trade, and create a fair playing field for businesses, consumers and workers.

Roosevelt earned the nickname "The Trust Buster" when a staggering 44 corporations were broken up during his administration. Using the Sherman Antitrust Act of 1890, he helped dismantle monopolies like the American Tobacco Company, Standard Oil, DuPont Chemical Corporation and Northern Securities Trust—which was formed by the Northwestern railroads to artificially hike transportation rates. That same year, he intervened in a bitter coal strike in Pennsylvania, using unique negotiation tactics to halt the action and gaining pay raises for American miners.

Roosevelt was driven to protect the American consumer against massive money-hungry

> ## "A GREAT DEMOCRACY HAS GOT TO BE PROGRESSIVE, OR IT WILL SOON CEASE TO BE EITHER GREAT OR A DEMOCRACY."
>
> THEODORE ROOSEVELT

DID YOU KNOW?
Roosevelt set a record for a head of state by shaking hands with 8,513 people at a White House function on January 1, 1907.

No stranger to tragedy, Roosevelt lost his wife and mother to illness on the same day in 1884.

BIRTH OF THE "TEDDY BEAR"

AMERICA'S MOST ENDURING CHILDREN'S TOY WAS NAMED AFTER THE CRUSTY "ROUGH RIDER"

In 1902, Teddy Roosevelt was on a bear-hunting trip in Mississippi. As it went on, Teddy was one of the few hunters yet to bag a bear, so the men in his party captured one and invited him to shoot the tied-up animal for his kill. But viewing the idea "unsportsmanlike," Roosevelt refused, inspiring a political cartoon that drew national attention—along with that of candy store owners Rose and Morris Michtom. They created a cuddly, stuffed bear cub, sent it to Roosevelt for approval and put it in the window of their Brooklyn, New York, store, calling it "Teddy's Bear." The stuffed bear captured America's imagination and was an immediate hit. Roosevelt himself even used a "Teddy Bear" as his mascot when he ran for reelection three years later.

businesses that were more interested in profits than the well-being of their consumers. Horrifying abuses in the meatpacking industry and rampant false advertising of so-called patent drugs with virtually no medicinal value inspired his efforts to protect consumers with his revolutionary Pure Food and Drug Act and the Meat Inspection Act in 1906.

The avid outdoorsman wielded his presidential powers to create the United States Forest Service after he was inspired by a 1903 camping trip to the Yosemite forest with environmentalist John Muir. During his administration, Roosevelt set aside 42 million acres for five national parks, 150 national forests, 55 bird sanctuaries and 18 national monuments. He used his executive powers liberally, once saying, "Is there any law that will prevent me from declaring Pelican Island a Federal Bird Reservation?.... Very well then, I so declare it!"

But it was internationally where he developed his reputation for "speaking softly and carrying a big stick"—he was more than willing to use force to back up his diplomatic negotiations. He pulled the Monroe Doctrine out of mothballs in 1904 to drive away European nations attempting to use force to collect debts from Latin American nations,

creating the Roosevelt Corollary, which stated that America was free to intervene in any affairs it deemed necessary in the Western Hemisphere. He declared Colombia a good place to start, carving out the new country of Panama and taking over the abandoned French construction of the Panama Canal, which would link the Atlantic and Pacific Oceans and enhance American trade and defense interests in the Far East, as well as in Central and South America. When completed, he called the canal his greatest accomplishment as president. He also struck an agreement with Japan that traded diplomatic recognition of that country in return for its acceptance of U.S. control of the Philippines.

Roosevelt, whose volunteer Rough Riders cavalry brigade charged up San Juan Hill to victory in Cuba in 1898 during the Spanish-American War, dedicated himself to making America a global military power. By the end of his presidency, the former assistant secretary of the Navy had fortified his fleet into a major international force at sea. He demonstrated the nation's newfound naval strength by sending his "Great White Fleet" around the world for two years between 1907 and 1909, sending the message that he would drop his big stick wherever needed. Yet he is also the same man who won the Nobel Peace Prize for brokering negotiations that ended the Russo-Japanese War.

Despite his fighting DNA, Roosevelt's administration was marked by reform, conservation, prosperity—and peace. In his book *Theodore Rex*, historian Edmund Morris says, "Few, if any Americans, could match the breadth of his intellect and the strength of his character."

After departing from the White House, Roosevelt noted, "When I left the presidency I finished seven-and-a-half years of administration, during which not one shot had been fired against a foreign foe. We were at absolute peace, and there was no nation in the world with whom a war cloud threatened, no nation in the world whom we had wronged, or from whom we had anything to fear."

1901–1909

BORN OCT. 27, 1858, NEW YORK CITY
DIED JAN. 6, 1919, OYSTER BAY, NEW YORK
BURIAL SITE SAGAMORE HILL, OYSTER BAY, NEW YORK
EDUCATION HARVARD UNIVERSITY
POLITICAL PARTY REPUBLICAN
AGE AT INAUGURATION 42
VICE PRESIDENT CHARLES W. FAIRBANKS (2ND TERM)
OPPONENT INAUGURATED AFTER McKINLEY WAS ASSASSINATED; ALTON B. PARKER (2ND TERM)
OCCUPATIONS BEFORE PRESIDENCY WRITER, HISTORIAN, POLITICIAN
OTHER OFFICES NEW YORK STATE ASSEMBLYMAN; U.S. CIVIL SERVICE COMMISSIONER; PRESIDENT OF NEW YORK BOARD OF POLICE COMMISSIONERS; ASSISTANT SECRETARY OF THE NAVY; GOVERNOR OF NEW YORK; U.S. VICE PRESIDENT
FIRST LADY EDITH KERMIT CAROW ROOSEVELT
NICKNAMES TR, THE TRUST BUSTER, TEDDY

ROOSEVELT'S "GREATEST ACCOMPLISHMENT"

France was the first to begin construction on the Panama Canal, but it was a disaster. Between January 1882 and 1888, when the project was abandoned, $287 million was spent and 20,000 workers lost their lives. That's when Roosevelt took over. In 1902, the U.S. bought the rights to the French canal property and equipment for $40 million. In 1903, Colombia signed a treaty allowing the U.S. to build the canal in a 6-mile-wide zone and use it for 100 years. In exchange, the U.S. would pay Colombia $10 million down and $250,000 a year. The Senate passed the treaty within two months. Then Colombia demanded more money. Roosevelt was ready to take military action, but instead supported a Panamanian independence revolution using an old treaty with Colombia against them. The U.S. immediately recognized Panama's independence and started negotiating a new treaty with them. It was almost the same as the one Colombia rejected, but this time, the canal zone would be over 9 miles wide.

The first ship passed through the Panama Canal on August 15, 1914, instantly giving the U.S. immediate access to the two oceans, maximizing trade opportunities and creating the ability to respond to military crises anywhere in the world in less than half the time as before.

WILLIAM HOWARD
TAFT

*A PRESIDENT WHO WAS BETTER SUITED FOR
THE JUDGE'S CHAMBERS THAN THE OVAL OFFICE*

★ ★ ★ ─────────────────────────

**RANKING
23**

WILLIAM HOWARD TAFT WAS NOT THEODORE ROOSEVELT, and he remained in his predecessor's shadows throughout his term. But that may not have bothered the "plodding legalistic" Taft; he might have been more interested in presiding over a courtroom than the bully pulpit.

Taft was a "reluctant" chief executive who never really wanted the job. He once exclaimed he would never become president, had no ambition of becoming president and "any party which would nominate me would make a great mistake." But Taft was an immensely gifted chief justice and the most judicial president, resolving everything by proselytizing the Constitution and defending the Founding Fathers' views of populist threats to American democracy.

He pledged to continue Roosevelt's reforms in his inauguration speech, but their relationship was about to get very chippy: Taft fired aides that were close to or even appointed by Roosevelt, including chief forester Gifford Pinchot, a well-respected conservationist.

Despite his lack of interest in the Oval Office, Taft followed through on some of the policies his party had promised. In his first message to Congress,

KEY ACHIEVEMENTS

- Broke up big businesses including Standard Oil Company and American Tobacco Company.

- Passed the eight-hour workday bill that stated federal employees shall work no longer than eight hours.

Taft proposed a 2 percent tax on the net income of all corporations except banks and proposed the 16th Amendment, permitting Congress to collect personal federal income taxes.

Trust-busting was at an all-time high under Taft. He prosecuted as many as 99 defendants while in office. The most noteworthy included the breakups of the Standard Oil Company of New Jersey and the American Tobacco Company. He also filed suit against U.S. Steel for violating the Sherman Act. The Payne-Aldrich Tariff Act of 1909 was passed into law at Taft's request for lower tariffs. But the bill did not have the support of most Democrats or progressive Republicans, and it hastened Taft's eventual loss in the election of 1912.

Biographer Jeffrey Rosen believes Taft's achievements in office deserve more credit. "He lowered the tariff for the first time since the 1890s, raised corporate taxes, protected more lands for environmental conservation than Roosevelt, brought more antitrust suits in one term than Roosevelt brought in two, convinced Congress to pass a Canadian Free Trade agreement, and kept the peace."

DID YOU KNOW?
Taft was the first and only person to be elected president of the United States and appointed to the Supreme Court.

1909–1913

BORN SEPT. 15, 1857, CINCINNATI, OHIO
DIED MARCH 8, 1930, WASHINGTON, D.C.
BURIAL SITE ARLINGTON NATIONAL CEMETERY, ARLINGTON, VIRGINIA
EDUCATION YALE COLLEGE, CINCINNATI LAW SCHOOL
POLITICAL PARTY REPUBLICAN
AGE AT INAUGURATION 51
VICE PRESIDENT JAMES SHERMAN
OPPONENT WILLIAM JENNINGS BRYAN
OCCUPATIONS BEFORE PRESIDENCY LAWYER, REPORTER, PROFESSOR, DEAN OF THE UNIVERSITY OF CINCINNATI LAW SCHOOL
OTHER OFFICES ASSISTANT PROSECUTING ATTORNEY, HAMILTON COUNTY, OHIO; OHIO SUPERIOR COURT JUDGE; U.S. SOLICITOR GENERAL; FEDERAL CIRCUIT COURT JUDGE; CIVIL GOVERNOR OF PHILIPPINES; SECRETARY OF WAR
FIRST LADY HELEN "NELLIE" HERRON TAFT
NICKNAMES BIG BILL, BIG LUB

Both Taft and his father, Alphonso, held the cabinet position of Secretary of War under separate administrations.

THOMAS WOODROW
WILSON

AFTER REMAINING NEUTRAL, WILSON ENTERED
WORLD WAR I, THEN TRIED TO CREATE WORLD PEACE

★ ★ ★

RANKING
8

DESPITE BEING DYSLEXIC AND STRUGGLING TO READ AS a child, Thomas Woodrow Wilson had a keen intellect, graduated from Princeton and went on to earn a PhD in government and history from Johns Hopkins University—the only president to have earned that advanced degree. An academic before he came into office, he taught at Bryn Mawr, Wesleyan and Princeton where, in 1902, he was elected university president. He was also a prolific writer, authoring eight books on government and the five-volume *History of the American People*.

Wilson's achievements in reforming and upgrading academics and policies at Princeton brought him to the attention of the Democratic party, who recruited him to run for governor of New Jersey in 1910 with a reformist platform, and he won. After implementing his progressive ideas in New Jersey, he entered the national race for president in 1912, with a New Freedom platform of limited government and progressive tariff-cutting policies against Republican incumbent William Howard Taft and third-party candidate (and former president) Theodore Roosevelt. Wilson won in a landslide.

> **KEY ACHIEVEMENTS**
>
> • Delivered his Fourteen Points to Congress, outlining his plan to end WWI.
>
> • Signed the Federal Reserve Act, overhauling the nation's banking system to safeguard America's financial institutions, the economy and the supply of U.S. currency.

A believer in Parliamentary government, Wilson's administration got off to a roaring start, reducing tariffs and establishing the Federal Reserve system of banking. He established the Federal Trade Commission, put regulations in place to prohibit child labor, and appointed his Secretary of State William Brandeis to the Supreme Court, as the first Jewish justice. Still, Wilson, a Southerner by birth, also held discriminatory racial views that tarnished his legacy—he allowed segregation to continue, and the number of African Americans employed by the federal government diminished.

When World War I started in 1914, Wilson, a steadfast isolationist, kept the U.S. out of it for two-and-a-half years, stating the nation's neutrality "does not express what America ought to feel. We are not trying to keep out of trouble; we are trying to preserve the foundations on which peace may be rebuilt." But on April 27, 1917, Wilson officially declared war on Germany, a delayed response to its repeated attacks on British passenger ships—most notably the *Lusitania*—and a more immediate response to the United Kingdom's interception

> "AMERICA IS NOT ANYTHING IF IT CONSISTS OF EACH OF US. IT IS SOMETHING ONLY IF IT CONSISTS OF ALL OF US."

WOODROW WILSON

Wilson was the first president since Andrew Jackson to have a foreign-born parent: His mother was English.

From left: French Premier Georges Clemenceau, Wilson and British Prime Minister David Lloyd George signed the Treaty of Versailles.

DID YOU KNOW?
Wilson maintained a flock of sheep on the lawn of the White House to generate wool for the war effort.

of a German telegraph offering Mexico financial support for an attack on Texas, New Mexico and Arizona. At the time, Wilson declared the war would "make the world safe for democracy."

While the war raged abroad, the women's suffrage movement gathered steam at home, and after Wilson was reelected to a second term, in 1917 suffragists picketed the White House demanding the noncommittal Wilson's support. The protest turned violent, with several women being arrested. Several women then conducted a hunger strike in prison, which shocked the president into action. In January 1918, Wilson declared his backing of women's right to vote and continued to fight for ratification of the 19th Amendment granting that right; it was finally ratified by the necessary two-thirds of the states on August 18, 1920.

Wartime brought about other significant changes in the policies that shaped daily American life. When the U.S. first entered WWI, the military was understaffed and ill-prepared. In May 1917,

President Wilson passed the Selective Service Act, which authorized the government to draft nearly 3 million men into the U.S. Army. These forces were supplemented by an additional 2 million volunteers. A growing, national anti-German sentiment fed President Wilson's own paranoia about German spies on U.S. soil. The Espionage Act of 1917 set about to penalize anyone for interfering with or dodging the military draft on the basis of aiding and abetting the enemy. As the war was ending in Europe, Wilson forewarned, "I can predict with absolute certainty that within another generation there will be another world war if the nations of the world do not concert the method by which to prevent it."

Wilson envisioned a new world order and peace based on several factors, including self-determination, rule chosen by citizens, open and transparent diplomacy, and a global governing body to make treaties and agreements. He spelled out this vision in his "Fourteen Points of Light" speech, the last of which set the groundwork for a new global League of Nations.

Those attending the Paris Peace Conference in 1919 embraced the idea and the League of Nations became part of the Treaty of Versailles, signed by Allied leaders on June 28, 1919. Unfortunately, the concessions Wilson made during the peace negotiations did not sit well with a newly elected Republican Congress back home. Dogged in his pursuit of American-led world peace, President Wilson embarked upon a national tour to gin up support for the Treaty of Versailles and America's membership in the League of Nations—not an easy task, as many Americans were resistant to the U.S. being responsible for solving Europe's post-war problems. The tour took a toll on Wilson's already compromised health and he suffered a serious stroke which left him partially disabled—the true magnitude of which was largely hidden from the public. While Wilson recovered, the

U.S. ratification of the Treaty of Versailles failed by seven votes in the Senate, meaning the U.S. was still officially at war with Germany.

The White House may have physically broken Wilson, but Saladin Ambar, political science professor at Rutgers University, says Wilson's vision of America playing a central role in a league of nations was inspiring and "it shaped much of American foreign policy for the remainder of the twentieth century," making him one of America's greatest presidents.

In 1920, President Wilson was awarded the Nobel Peace Prize for his role as architect of the League of Nations. It wasn't until a year later—just months after Wilson left office—that the U.S. finally decreed an end to the war with Germany in the Knox-Porter Resolution and signing of the U.S.-German Peace Treaty. Though the U.S. never joined the League of Nations, the United Nations, formed in 1945, is certainly a part of Wilson's impressive legacy.

The 19th Amendment granted U.S. women the right to vote.

MR. PRESIDENT HOW LONG MUST WOMEN WAIT FOR LIBERTY?

1913–1921

BORN DEC. 28, 1856, STAUNTON, VIRGINIA
DIED FEB. 3, 1924, WASHINGTON, D.C.
BURIAL SITE NATIONAL CATHEDRAL, WASHINGTON, D.C.
EDUCATION COLLEGE OF NEW JERSEY (NOW PRINCETON UNIVERSITY)
POLITICAL PARTY DEMOCRATIC
AGE AT INAUGURATION 56
VICE PRESIDENT THOMAS R. MARSHALL
OPPONENTS THEODORE ROOSEVELT, WILLIAM HOWARD TAFT (1ST TERM); CHARLES HUGHES, ALAN BENSON (2ND TERM)
OCCUPATIONS BEFORE PRESIDENCY LAWYER, PROFESSOR AND PRESIDENT OF PRINCETON, AUTHOR
OTHER OFFICES GOVERNOR OF NEW JERSEY
FIRST LADIES ELLEN LOUISE AXSON WILSON (DIED AUG. 6, 1914); EDITH BOLLING GALT WILSON
NICKNAME SCHOOLMASTER IN POLITICS

WARREN GAMALIEL
HARDING

DESPITE LOOKING GOOD, HIS PRESIDENCY WAS UGLY

★ ★ ★

RANKING
39

THE FIRST OF ONLY THREE U.S. SENATORS TO GO DIRECTLY from the Senate to the White House (John F. Kennedy and Barack Obama are the other two), Warren Harding won the 1920 election in a landslide over Ohio Governor James M. Cox. He garnered 404 electoral votes and 16,143,407 popular votes, the largest percentage of the popular vote since the beginning of the two-party system. But Harding didn't seem too interested in making a big deal of it.

The day after his victory, Harding, rather than getting to work to vet Cabinet members, announced he was taking a vacation. He went to Texas to fish, golf—which he was lousy at, according to Harding biographer John W. Dean—and play poker; then, a cruise to Panama.

Harding's administration was mired by scandal, starting with the Teapot Dome Scandal in 1922. The *Wall Street Journal* reported Secretary of the Interior Albert B. Fall made a secret arrangement to lease the U.S. naval petroleum reserve at Wyoming's Teapot Dome to a private oil company. He was later found guilty of taking bribes and became the first U.S. Cabinet member to be convicted of crimes committed while in office.

KEY ACHIEVEMENTS

• Signed the Budget and Accounting Act in order to better organize the federal government's accounts.

• Signed the Sheppard-Towner Maternity and Infancy Act, granting matching federal funds to states for maternity and child care.

It wasn't all bad during Harding's 881 days in office, the fourth-shortest presidency. In 1921 Harding signed the Sheppard-Towner Maternity and Infancy Act, which issued federal funds for the health care of mothers and children.

Also on Harding's watch, the 19th Amendment was deemed constitutional by the Supreme Court, effectively guaranteeing women's suffrage.

Harding's presidency came to a rather abrupt end in August 1923. While traveling to Alaska and the West on his "voyage of understanding" tour to help improve his image, he suffered ptomaine poisoning—now called food poisoning—and developed pneumonia. He initially recovered, but the travel had exhausted him and he passed away, likely of a heart attack, in a San Francisco hotel room with first lady Florence Harding by his side.

American scholar Henry Julian Abraham described Harding as "one of the post's crassest failures to date" and "patently unqualified to serve as president." Harding himself agreed: "I am not fit for this office and should never have been here."

DID YOU KNOW?
Harding received an endorsement from entertainer Al Jolson when he ran for president.

1921–1923

BORN NOV. 2, 1865, BLOOMINGTON GROVE, OHIO
DIED AUG. 2, 1923, SAN FRANCISCO, CALIFORNIA
BURIAL SITE HARDING MEMORIAL PARK, MARION, OHIO
EDUCATION OHIO CENTRAL COLLEGE
POLITICAL PARTY REPUBLICAN
AGE AT INAUGURATION 55
VICE PRESIDENT CALVIN COOLIDGE
OPPONENT JAMES M. COX
OCCUPATIONS BEFORE PRESIDENCY NEWSPAPER EDITOR, TEACHER, INSURANCE SALESMAN, REPORTER, PUBLISHER
OTHER OFFICES MEMBER OF OHIO SENATE; LIEUTENANT GOVERNOR OF OHIO; U.S. SENATOR
FIRST LADY FLORENCE "FLOSSIE" MABEL KLING HARDING
NICKNAME WINNIE

As a senator, Harding missed two-thirds of the votes held during his tenure.

CALVIN
COOLIDGE

THE ECONOMY WAS SO GOOD, IT'S HARD TO RECALL
IF COOLIDGE ACTUALLY DID ANYTHING

★ ★ ★

RANKING
28

MOST AMERICANS TODAY MAY NOT KNOW HOW BEST to describe Calvin Coolidge's legacy, as his accomplishments of maintaining postwar peace and economic prosperity during the roaring twenties were overshadowed by the stock market crash of 1929, the ensuing Great Depression and Franklin D. Roosevelt's progressive New Deal.

While vacationing in Vermont in the summer of 1923, then-Vice President Coolidge was thrust into the presidency when President Warren G. Harding passed away in San Francisco in the midst of a cross-country tour.

A New Englander who had served as governor of Massachusetts, Coolidge shared and supported Harding's "return to normalcy" and laissez-faire policies, which he sustained throughout his own administration. In his first 15 months as president, Coolidge leaned into his Yankee sensibility of "living within your means" and his faith-based belief that financial wealth and material gain would ultimately establish a stronger moral fiber in both the individual and the American collective. That's a sharp contrast to the wanton extravagance and loosening of social and cultural norms that have defined the 1920s.

KEY ACHIEVEMENTS

- Per capita income rose from $522 in 1921 to $716 by 1929.
- National debt dropped from $22.3 billion in 1923 to $16.9 billion by 1926.
- Signed the Indian Citizenship Act, granting full U.S. citizenship to the indigenous people of the United States.

In his first message to Congress on December 6, 1923, Coolidge's primary goal was to institute tax policies to encourage investment and spur growth of the stock market. Following in the footsteps of former Presidents Woodrow Wilson and Harding, Coolidge also outlined an isolationist approach to foreign policy, contending that the U.S. will "attend to our own affairs, conserve our own strength, and protect the interests of our own citizens."

The success of his brief first term teed Coolidge up for election in 1924 by encouraging voters to "Keep Cool With Coolidge." The first order of business was to make good on his campaign promise of building upon the policies initiated by Harding: reduce taxes, reduce federal spending, pay down the national debt, reform tariffs.

Expanding on the success of the Revenue Act of 1924, deeper federal tax cuts were implemented with the Revenue Acts of 1926 and 1928. These ongoing tax reductions positively impacted all facets of the U.S. economy by increasing incentives for Americans to work, for American businesses and manufacturers to produce more, and for Americans to ultimately

Coolidge is the only president who was born on July 4.

DID YOU KNOW?
Coolidge was the first president to address the nation via radio in his State of the Union.

1923-1929

BORN JULY 4, 1872, PLYMOUTH NOTCH, VERMONT
DIED JAN. 5, 1933, NORTHAMPTON, MASSACHUSETTS
BURIAL SITE HILLSIDE CEMETERY, PLYMOUTH, VERMONT
EDUCATION AMHERST COLLEGE
POLITICAL PARTY REPUBLICAN
AGE AT INAUGURATION 51
VICE PRESIDENT CHARLES G. DAWES (2ND TERM)
OPPONENTS JOHN DAVIS; ROBERT LA FOLLETTE
OCCUPATION BEFORE PRESIDENCY LAWYER
OTHER OFFICES MEMBER OF THE U.S. HOUSE OF REPRESENTATIVES; MAYOR OF NORTHAMPTON, MASSACHUSETTS; MEMBER AND PRESIDENT OF MASSACHUSETTS SENATE; LIEUTENANT GOVERNOR OF MASSACHUSETTS; GOVERNOR OF MASSACHUSETTS; U.S. VICE PRESIDENT
FIRST LADY GRACE GOODHUE COOLIDGE
NICKNAME SILENT CAL

buy more. Between 1924 and 1929, gross domestic product rose from $85.2 billion to $101.4 billion.

Despite the accomplishments of his administration, a pall hung over the latter half of his reelection campaign and presidency. As he grew ever more distant and disconnected, contemporaries and historians alike attributed Coolidge's apathy to a lifelong bout with clinical depression that was reignited by the sudden death (due to sepsis) of his youngest son, Calvin Jr., at 16.

In 1927, while vacationing in South Dakota, the milquetoast "Silent Cal" announced he would not seek a second term as president with a simple, succinct statement: "I do not choose to run for president in 1928."

HERBERT CLARK
HOOVER

THE GREAT DEPRESSION WAS TOO MUCH FOR HOOVER TO OVERCOME

★ ★ ☆

RANKING
35

UNDER HERBERT HOOVER'S PREDECESSOR, CALVIN Coolidge, the Roaring Twenties were marked with unprecedented expansion in the stock market, creating an unsustainable bubble of assets. Then it burst. Scholars agree that exuberant and unregulated speculation—with citizens from all economic backgrounds having access to easy credit lines to borrow money to buy stocks "on margin"—and a drought that caused an agricultural crisis, were two major contributors to the Black Tuesday stock market crash on October 29, 1929; by December 1, New York Stock Exchange stocks had lost $26 billion in value, and within a year nearly 1,300 banks closed.

A Stanford-educated son of a blacksmith, Hoover had earned a reputation as a noble humanitarian who had mobilized a successful relief effort in 1921 to help millions of citizens in World War I–ravaged Belgium. He'd gone on to serve as the head of the Food Administration, and continued his good works as head of the American Relief Administration where, after sending food aid to famine-stricken Russia, he retorted to a critic,

KEY ACHIEVEMENTS

- Got Congress to fund $116 million in public works projects for 4.5 million unemployed.

- Increased the federal budget for children's programs, including health care for the physically and mentally handicapped and prenatal care.

- Increased funding for national parks and added 3 million acres to the national park inventory.

"Twenty million people are starving. Whatever their politics, they shall be fed!" But once in the Oval Office, he felt that assistance should be handled on a local, voluntary basis.

As the economic turmoil worsened through 1930 and 1931, and the country became more entrenched in debt ($17 billion at the start of the Depression), malnutrition and unemployment (4.5 million), Hoover vetoed relief bills for struggling Americans and rejected calls for aggressive government action, believing that excessive federal intervention would threaten capitalism. In his 1930 State of the Union address, Hoover explained that "prosperity cannot be restored by raids upon the public Treasury."

He did, however, get Congress to vote to fund $116 million in public works projects to alleviate the escalating unemployment, including the construction of the Hoover Dam. And in the fall of 1931, he formed the President's Emergency Committee on Employment to coordinate private organizations' efforts to help unemployed workers.

DID YOU KNOW?
Hoover lived in London during World War I and helped evacuate 120,000 Americans trapped in Europe.

Orphaned at age 9, Hoover became a millionaire after working as a leading mining engineer.

1929–1933

BORN AUG. 10, 1874, WEST BRANCH, IOWA
DIED OCT. 20, 1964, NEW YORK, NEW YORK
BURIAL SITE HOOVER PRESIDENTIAL LIBRARY, WEST BRANCH, IOWA
EDUCATION STANFORD UNIVERSITY
POLITICAL PARTY REPUBLICAN
AGE AT INAUGURATION 54
VICE PRESIDENT CHARLES CURTIS
OPPONENT ALFRED E. SMITH
OCCUPATION BEFORE PRESIDENCY MINING ENGINEER
OTHER OFFICES CHAIRMAN OF COMMISSION FOR RELIEF IN BELGIUM; U.S. FOOD ADMINISTRATOR; CHAIRMAN OF SUPREME ECONOMIC COUNCIL; SECRETARY OF COMMERCE
FIRST LADY LOU HENRY HOOVER
NICKNAMES THE CHIEF, THE GREAT ENGINEER

In his memoirs, Hoover wrote that the Great Depression did not start in the United States: "To be sure, we were due for some economic readjustment as a result of the orgy of stock speculation in 1928–1929. This orgy was not a consequence of my administrative policies."

In *Hoover and The Historians: The Resurrection of a President*, Patrick G. O'Brien and Philip T. Rosen acknowledge that Hoover was a man highly regarded when elected, and then vilified by the public by the end of his term, stating, "the textbook interpretations of Hoover ranged from highly critical through ambivalent to almost nonexistent."

MEMORABLE FIRST
LADIES

AMERICA'S PRESIDENTIAL PARTNERS HAVE BEEN
BELOVED INSPIRATIONS TO THE COUNTRY

★ ★ ★

Martha Jefferson Randolph informally took on the role of first lady for her father.

THE ROLE OF THE FIRST LADY OF THE UNITED STATES IS unpaid and historically underappreciated, yet comes with many unofficial duties, including that of gracious hostess. While some preferred to remain behind the scenes, supporting their husbands quietly from the shadows, others arrived at the White House already accomplished in their own right and took their place by their husbands' sides to help shape America's policy. Here, a look at a few of the more notable players.

Martha Jefferson Randolph
First daughter, 1801–1809

Thomas Jefferson's daughter was only 10 years old when her mother, Martha, died. The first daughter—and Jefferson's only child—became her father's chief consoler, companion and confidante. As a teenager, she traveled with him to France, where she studied needlework, painting, history and Latin. Their close bond made it natural for Martha to serve as Jefferson's companion while he presided over official state business.

Julia Boggs Dent Grant
1869–1877

Ulysses S. Grant's wife, Julia, was not your typical lady of high society. Though she was born in 1826 to affluent slaveholder parents on a plantation

HIGH MARKS
Michelle Obama had a 68 percent approval rating when she left office in 2017.

First lady Julia Grant may have saved her husband from assassination.

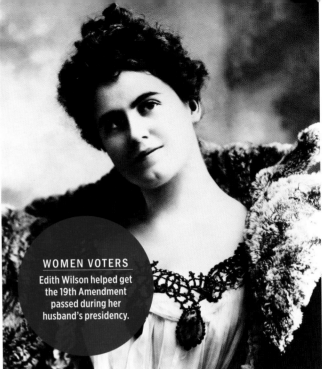

WOMEN VOTERS
Edith Wilson helped get the 19th Amendment passed during her husband's presidency.

outside of St. Louis and attended boarding school, she was an accomplished pianist and voracious reader who often preferred fishing and horseback riding with her brothers. Known for being direct, candid and at times willful, Grant was perceived as a breath of fresh air among the Washington, D.C., elite. She eschewed the more frugal ways of her predecessor, Mary Todd Lincoln, and instead spent lavishly on White House decor and hosting 29-course dinners. Having grown up with slaves, Julia was somewhat delusional about the quality of life experienced by slaves, including after emancipation. She is said to have believed they were truly happy with their stations in life and continued to rely on the aid of at least one slave, also named Julia, during the Civil War while her husband was leading the Union in its mission to free them. As the Civil War was nearing its end,

a highly publicized rift between Julia and then first lady Mary Lincoln broke out at a Virginia military camp. But it's this animosity that may have ultimately saved the general's life: The Grants were invited to join the Lincolns at the Ford Theatre on that fateful night in 1865, but did not attend. It's believed that John Wilkes Booth and his co-conspirators had also targeted Grant for assassination for his role in the abolition of slavery.

Edith Bolling Galt Wilson
1915–1921

In her role as first lady, Woodrow Wilson's second wife, Edith, was her husband's confidante and gatekeeper, diligently screening both his mail and his visitors while he navigated the U.S. through World War I. She often sat in on presidential meetings with political leaders and foreign representatives. In 1918, while serving his second term, the president experienced a paralyzing stroke. Edith was determined to keep his position intact and launched a campaign of misinformation intended to mislead Congress and the public into believing that her husband was only suffering from temporary exhaustion, which required extensive rest. For the remainder of Wilson's presidency, Edith ran the country from behind the scenes, decoding diplomatic and military messages sent from Europe for her husband during World War I—much to the dismay of his administration and Congress.

Eleanor Rosalynn Smith Carter
1977–1981

Nicknamed "Steel Magnolia" for her combination of sweet Southern charm and strong will, Jimmy Carter's wife, Rosalynn, was instrumental in her husband's entire political career. During Carter's presidency, Rosalynn participated in Cabinet meetings, weighed in on policy decisions as the voice of the people and even made her own campaign promise—that as America's first lady, she would dedicate time and energy to national mental health legislation. She, along with the United Nations, helped to raise millions of dollars in aid for Cambodian refugees who fled mass genocide inflicted by the Khmer Rouge.

Michelle Robinson Obama
2009–2017

Princeton. Harvard Law School. Sidley Austin LLP. University of Chicago. Michelle's academic and professional path before she became the first African American first lady in U.S. history rivals that of her husband, Barack Obama. And as the only first lady in American history to hold two Ivy League degrees, some say it's even more impressive. During her eight years in the White House, the self-proclaimed "mom in chief" never lost sight of her core values: family first, physical health and well-being, and education. As first lady, she launched the Let's Move! campaign, targeting the growing childhood obesity epidemic, saying, "The physical and emotional health of an entire generation and the economic health and security of our nation is at stake." In 2017, when President and Mrs. Obama left office, Michelle had a 68 percent favorable approval rating among her fellow Americans.

Rosalynn Carter was instrumental in her husband's political career.

FRANKLIN DELANO
ROOSEVELT

FDR DEALT WITH THE GREAT DEPRESSION AND WORLD WAR II.
HE LED, HE FOUGHT — HE WAS THIS COUNTRY'S SAVIOR

★ ★ ★

RANKING
3

FRANKLIN DELANO ROOSEVELT WAS CONSIDERED A "SICKLY child," as noted in nearly every biography. Yet he grew up to be the greatest American president in terms of accomplishments, successfully straddling two of the most seismic periods of human history—something his other great predecessors didn't have to deal with. As author and historian Robert Dallek pointed out: "George Washington sets the nation on its democratic path. Abraham Lincoln preserves it. Franklin Roosevelt sees the nation through the Depression and war."

Roosevelt took America out of the Great Depression and engineered the country's decisive role in the Allies winning the Second World War. In an unprecedented (and now, by law, impossible to repeat) four terms as president, he also created Social Security and the New Deal, the bedrock of modern America. He brought about banking reform, set up agencies to support farmers and help employ those left out of work by the Great Depression— 13 million at the time of his first inauguration— regulated the stock market, instituted bank-deposit insurance and subsidized home mortgages, and ended Prohibition. He helped to re-instill public trust in government through his Fireside Chats. (He also created the first significant federal deficit, if you want to nitpick.)

And he did all of this while desperately afflicted by polio, having picked up the virus while he was on vacation in 1921.

Yet despite his success in helping to turn the nation around, "early survey researchers noted in 1936 that 83 percent of Republicans believed that Roosevelt's policies were leading the country down the road to dictatorship, a view shared by only 9 percent of Democrats," according to political scientist Donald P. Green, co-author of *Partisan Hearts and Minds: Political Parties and the Social Identities of Voters.*

Roosevelt, a large man who stood 6 feet 2 inches tall, was a huge personality, but he walked a tightrope when World War II broke out in Europe in 1939 after Adolf Hitler invaded Poland. The Depression hadn't just affected the U.S.; it also impacted the rest of the world, especially in Europe, where a wave of rising far-right nationalism brought Hitler and Mussolini to power on a hatred

KEY ACHIEVEMENTS

- Shepherded 15 major bills in his first 105 days to get America recovering from the Great Depression, including the creation of Civilian Conservation Corps, which created jobs.

- Created Social Security.

- Led the United States into World War II.

> ## "MEETING HIM IS LIKE OPENING A BOTTLE OF CHAMPAGNE."
>
> WINSTON CHURCHILL, ON ROOSEVELT

Urged on by his wife, Eleanor, FDR appointed more women to federal posts than any previous president (including the first woman to a cabinet post).

DID YOU KNOW?
Roosevelt was an enthusiastic philatelist. At his death, his personal collection numbered over 1.2 million stamps.

Throughout his presidency, Roosevelt spent time each day with his stamp collection.

of outsiders. As war in Europe became inevitable, it was clear to FDR that in the U.S. there was an overwhelming public desire to stay out of it. And so he did. He asserted that the U.S. would adopt a so-called "good neighbor" policy whereby the U.S. would assist its allies who were at war with the Axis powers—Germany, Italy and Japan—with weapons and supplies, but stay out of the conflict militarily. He famously resisted British Prime Minister Winston Churchill's entreaties to join the fight.

But that soon changed. "Yesterday, December 7, 1941—a date which will live in infamy—the United States of America was suddenly and deliberately attacked by naval and air forces of the Empire of Japan," Roosevelt announced of the attack on Pearl Harbor as the country moved to war. Soon the Germans and Italians, somewhat redundantly, declared war on the U.S. Upon entering the war, Roosevelt created what he called "a grand alliance" that would eventually become the United Nations. His objective was to have all the nations fighting

1933–1945

BORN JAN. 30, 1882, HYDE PARK, NEW YORK
DIED APRIL 12, 1945, WARM SPRINGS, GEORGIA
BURIAL SITE HYDE PARK, NEW YORK
EDUCATION HARVARD UNIVERSITY
POLITICAL PARTY DEMOCRATIC
AGE AT INAUGURATION 51
VICE PRESIDENTS JOHN N. GARNER (1ST AND 2ND TERMS); HENRY A. WALLACE (3RD TERM), HARRY S. TRUMAN (4TH TERM)
OPPONENTS HERBERT HOOVER (1ST TERM); ALFRED LANDON (2ND TERM); WENDELL WILLKIE (3RD TERM); THOMAS E. DEWEY (4TH TERM)
OCCUPATIONS BEFORE PRESIDENCY LAWYER, POLITICIAN
OTHER OFFICES MEMBER OF NEW YORK STATE SENATE; ASSISTANT SECRETARY OF THE NAVY; GOVERNOR OF NEW YORK
FIRST LADY ELEANOR ROOSEVELT
NICKNAMES FDR, THE SPHINX

Hitler and his allies in agreement, not to make a separate peace with them, and to participate in a peacekeeping force after the war was won, as he confidently believed would happen.

FDR did not direct America's part in the war as closely and with as much involvement as Churchill did. He installed key generals in significant roles, most notably Dwight D. Eisenhower, George S. Patton, Omar Bradley and Douglas MacArthur, who turned the war around at a time when it was going terribly for the Allies. Roosevelt's main focus was the bigger political picture, ultimately resulting in the Yalta Conference in Crimea (then part of the Soviet Union) in 1945, which drew up the lines of postwar Europe in the (correct) expectation that the war would soon end victoriously for the Allies.

In 2017, NPR's Ron Elving said of FDR—who oversaw the planning for D-Day, June 6, 1944, as part of his grand strategy—that his "contribution to the war was also largely his extraordinary ability to handle people, including the world's most difficult people."

In the beginning, Roosevelt didn't send U.S. forces to Europe, wanting to instead gain fighting experience and conditioning for his troops in North Africa, where the Allies routed the Germans and then invaded Sicily and Italy. This cautious approach seeded the great distrust the Soviets felt for the West, because Joseph Stalin—then premier of the Soviet Union—felt the Allies were fighting the war disproportionately with Russian lives, 9 million of which were lost repelling the Nazis. And historians believe that distrust later led to the Cold War.

By the end of war in both Europe and against the Japanese in the Pacific, 405,000 American soldiers lost their lives fighting for what Roosevelt called the "Four universal human freedoms—freedom of speech, freedom of religion, freedom from want and freedom from fear." Sadly, those freedoms didn't apply to Japanese Americans living in the U.S. at the time, and Roosevelt, again following the public mood, wrote Executive Order 9066 to put 112,000 of them in the infamous internment camps.

THE MYSTERIOUS TRACK 61

ONE OF NEW YORK'S MOST FAMOUS HOTELS HAD A SECRET ENTRANCE FOR FDR

One of New York City's best-kept secrets is the existence of a train station under the legendary Waldorf Astoria Hotel; the station is an extension of Grand Central Terminal, located a few blocks away.

Roosevelt commissioned the station so he could discreetly travel from D.C. directly to the hotel without being noticed, since he was stricken with polio—and to most of America that was still a secret.

Every president since has used the station to access the hotel, which is a big part of why they stay there rather than at, frankly, more luxurious hotels.

FDR's train, with its gun turrets and a special car for his limousine, remains in the station today. And there is only one sign of the station on the street, which millions of people pass without ever noticing: a nondescript exit elevator with the curious address of 101-121 East 49th Street.

FDR checked into the hotel without being checked out.

In October 1941, two months before Pearl Harbor and the U.S. entry into the war, Roosevelt approved the Manhattan Project, the top-secret undertaking to build an atomic bomb. FDR had learned, through a letter from Albert Einstein, that Hitler was trying to develop this devastating weapon himself and would in all likelihood eventually use it. Roosevelt realized this was a race that the United States simply had to win. The project was kept so hush-hush, despite some 100,000 people working on it at any given time, that when Vice President Harry S. Truman became president following Roosevelt's death four years later, he himself had to be briefed on it from top military aides.

On April 12, 1945, just a few months after being inaugurated into his fourth term, Roosevelt suffered a massive stroke while he was away on vacation at his retreat in Warm Springs, Georgia, passing away only a couple of hours later. Upon his death, Ohio's Republican Senator Robert Taft, a longtime foe of FDR, said his death "removes the greatest figure of our time."

In his tenure, FDR lifted America from some of its darkest hours and delivered it to the dawn of its brightest time.

DEAL OF THE CENTURY

FDR'S NEW DEAL CREATED JOBS AND A PROSPEROUS ECONOMY, AND ESTABLISHED STABILITY

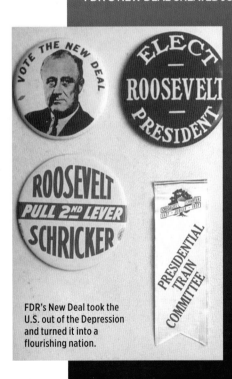

FDR's New Deal took the U.S. out of the Depression and turned it into a flourishing nation.

Simply put, the New Deal effectively ended the Depression. (World War II and the massive increase in weapons manufacturing was the final spur to economic recovery.) And it created the modern United States, with a far more powerful and stable society.

Roosevelt realized that the government had to act decisively and innovatively to rebuild people's lives. Within the first 100 days of his administration, he first temporarily closed the banks to halt depositor withdrawals, and then reorganized them and restored public confidence in the system. He mandated that unstable banks be shut, culling a sickly herd of institutions. He created the Tennessee Valley Authority, which built dams to control flooding and create hydroelectric power for most of the South. He convinced Congress to pass a bill that paid farmers to not produce certain products, thus reducing surpluses and increasing prices to heal what was still principally an agricultural economy. He helped pass the National Industrial Recovery Act, which allowed for collective bargaining to increase wages and improve worker rights, and brought more than a dozen other productive reforms to light.

Perhaps most remarkably, Roosevelt spurred Congress to act—maybe the surest measure of his greatness as a leader.

FDR showed his leadership skills in war and peace. Clockwise from top left: With Winston Churchill and Joseph Stalin at Yalta in 1945; the Japanese attack on Pearl Harbor in 1941; signing the Social Security Bill in 1935; the 1944 D-Day invasion.

HARRY S.
TRUMAN

TRUMAN'S FIERY GRIT CEMENTED HIS PLACE AS ONE OF THE FINEST COMMANDERS IN CHIEF

★ ★ ★ ──────────────────────────────

RANKING
6

WHEN HARRY TRUMAN OFFERED COMFORT TO ELEANOR Roosevelt after her husband, Franklin, died 82 days into his fourth term, she looked at the new president and famously replied, "Is there anything we can do for you? You are the one in trouble now."

"The first four months of his administration were the most challenging four-month period of any president," said A.J. Baime, author of *The Accidental President.* "He oversaw the collapse of Nazi Germany, the victory at Okinawa, the dropping of the atomic bombs, the founding of the United Nations, the Potsdam Conference where he negotiated the new map of the world with [British Prime Minister Winston] Churchill and [Soviet Communist Party General Secretary Joseph] Stalin, and the dawn of the Cold War. At the end of all this, Americans had achieved a sense of unity that is unimaginable today."

Just a month after FDR's death, a victory over Germany was secured, but Truman was left with the horrific dilemma of whether to drop the atomic bomb in order to avoid a bloody invasion of Japan. His decision to drop A-bombs on Hiroshima and Nagasaki created an estimated death toll of 246,000 Japanese, but likely saved millions more lives on both sides. It was a decision he struggled with, but never doubted, asserting, "It is part of my responsibility as commander in chief of the armed forces to see to it that our country is able to defend itself against any possible aggressor."

And when North Korea invaded the South on June 25, 1950, the warrior in Truman reemerged, sending in troops to push them back. When fabled Gen. Douglas MacArthur publicly discounted Truman's order not to follow them past the 38th Parallel into the North, a furious Truman boldly fired the popular war hero for "rank insubordination," and relieved him of his duties, ordering him home. "I fired MacArthur because he wouldn't respect the authority of the president.

> **KEY ACHIEVEMENTS**
>
> • His Marshall Plan helped rebuild and stimulate economic recovery in Western Europe.
>
> • Provided supplies to West Berliners in 1948, one of the first major victories of the Cold War.
>
> • Was a driving force in the formation of both the United Nations and NATO.

"IF YOU CAN'T STAND THE HEAT, GET OUT OF THE KITCHEN."

HARRY S. TRUMAN

In 1947, Truman became the first president to deliver a speech on live television.

DID YOU KNOW?
Truman was the only president in the 20th century who did not attend college.

WHATEVER HAPPENED TO DEWEY?

THE MULTI-TIME PRESIDENTIAL CANDIDATE TOOK A LICKING FROM POLITICIANS AND MOBSTERS

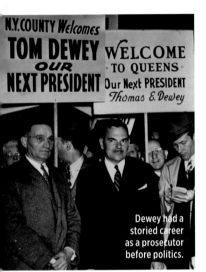

Dewey had a storied career as a prosecutor before politics.

Thomas E. Dewey not only didn't defeat Truman in 1948 (despite what the newspapers said…), he'd also gotten crushed in the presidential election by Franklin Delano Roosevelt four years earlier!

While it would be unfair to label the three-term governor of New York a two-time loser, his career, which began with much fanfare, ended under a cloud.

Dewey started as a crusading prosecutor who went after massive mob figures, such as Al Capone. When he targeted notorious gangster "Dutch" Schultz, the mobster put out a $10,000 contract on Dewey—but organized crime group Murder, Inc. took out Schultz instead. In later years, rumors swirled around the governor claiming that he had started making deals with the mob, including giving notorious gangster Charles "Lucky" Luciano a mysterious pardon.

Dewey continued his role as a Republican leader into the late 1960s, when President Richard Nixon offered him the position of chief justice of the United States; he declined because he thought he was too old for the job. He was due to attend the engagement party of Nixon's daughter Tricia on March 16, 1971, but was found lying dead on his hotel room bed, age 68.

I didn't fire him because he was a dumb son of a b----, although he was," Truman declared.

Truman's move drew heavy criticism, lowering his approval rating to just 22 percent. "A record not matched before or ever since…lower even than Nixon's at the depth of the Watergate scandal," said H.W. Brands, author of *The General vs. the President: MacArthur and Truman at the Brink of Nuclear War*. But despite the blow to his popularity, Truman is now credited with achieving his goals of driving the Communist troops out of South Korea—which has lived under a democratic government ever since.

Truman decided against running for reelection in 1952, and when he left the White House he was one of the most unpopular politicians in the U.S. But in time, his reputation has been rehabilitated, and many now see him as a symbol of plainspoken Midwestern common sense, who kept the country going through some of its most difficult times.

1945–1953

BORN MAY 8, 1884, LAMAR, MISSOURI
DIED DEC. 26, 1972, KANSAS CITY, MISSOURI
BURIAL SITE INDEPENDENCE, MISSOURI
EDUCATION NO FORMAL DEGREES
POLITICAL PARTY DEMOCRATIC
AGE AT INAUGURATION 60
VICE PRESIDENT ALBEN W. BARKLEY
OPPONENT THOMAS E. DEWEY
OCCUPATIONS BEFORE PRESIDENCY RAILROAD TIMEKEEPER, BANK CLERK, FARMER, HABERDASHER
OTHER OFFICES COUNTY JUDGE FOR EASTERN DISTRICT OF JACKSON COUNTY, MISSOURI; PRESIDING JUDGE, COUNTY COURT, JACKSON COUNTY, MISSOURI; UNITED STATES SENATOR; U.S. VICE PRESIDENT
FIRST LADY ELIZABETH "BESS" WALLACE TRUMAN
NICKNAME GIVE 'EM HELL HARRY

After taking office in 1945, Truman first focused on ending World War II. Clockwise from top left: Addressing the United Nations in June; with Churchill and Stalin at the Potsdam Conference in July; the atomic bomb at Hiroshima on August 6; with the Japanese Instrument of Surrender on September 2.

DWIGHT D.
EISENHOWER

A SOLDIER OF GOOD FORTUNE, IKE WAS BORN TO LEAD ON AND OFF THE BATTLEFIELD

★ ★ ★

**RANKING
7**

THE SON OF PACIFISTS, DWIGHT D. EISENHOWER graduated from West Point in 1915 and went on to an extraordinary military career before being elected as the commander in chief in 1952. Despite his victories in pivotal battles during World War II, however, as president he often promoted the lessons he had learned early in life from his peace-loving parents. "No people on Earth can be held, as a people, to be enemy," he said in a 1953 speech, "for all humanity shares the common hunger for peace and fellowship and justice."

Nevertheless, Eisenhower paid his dues in the Army, rising through the ranks first as an aide to legendary World War I Commander Gen. John J. Pershing, and later to U.S. Army Chief of Staff Gen. Douglas MacArthur. By September 1941, Eisenhower had become a brigadier general and would be the man who was largely responsible for some of America's greatest WWII victories.

In November 1942, Eisenhower led the invasion of North Africa called Operation Torch, the largest amphibious invasion the world had ever seen. The following July, he took the reins of the invasion of Sicily, called Operation Husky, which was even larger than Torch. After being promoted to supreme commander of the Allied Expeditionary Forces, Eisenhower was directed by President Roosevelt to command Operation Overlord and invade Europe. The Normandy landing of D-Day on June 6, 1944, is still the largest invasion in history; it led to the liberation of Paris and turned the tide of the entire war.

In less than two years, Eisenhower's military operations collectively and stunningly ended the Nazi stranglehold on Western Europe—a feat Jean Edward Smith, author of *Eisenhower in War and Peace*, called "unprecedented in the history of warfare."

Still, his own words following the victories revealed a remarkable distaste for his unequaled abilities in combat. "I hate war as only a soldier who has lived it can," Eisenhower said, "only as one who has seen its brutality, its futility, its stupidity."

After the war, Eisenhower was pulled out of private life by President Truman to head North Atlantic Treaty Organization (NATO) forces in Europe. Republicans then drafted him to become their presidential candidate in 1952. During his campaign against Democratic candidate Adlai Stevenson, Eisenhower rode around the country by train, speaking plainly from the steps of the caboose, and the phrase "I like Ike," entered the national lexicon. On election day, Eisenhower won big.

> **KEY ACHIEVEMENTS**
> • Authorized the creation of NASA.
> • Renovated the country's infrastructure with the Federal Highway Act.
> • Pushed through the Civil Rights Act of 1957.

DID YOU KNOW?

Eisenhower changed the name of Camp David from Shangri-La to honor both his father, David Jacob, and his grandson Dwight David (who later married Richard Nixon's daughter Julie).

Eisenhower had a small art studio in the White House, where he would try to spend a few minutes each day painting.

"LEADERSHIP IS THE ART OF GETTING SOMEONE ELSE TO DO SOMETHING YOU WANT DONE BECAUSE HE WANTS TO DO IT."

DWIGHT EISENHOWER

After becoming president, Eisenhower focused on peace efforts as commander in chief. It was left to him to formally end another war, and he negotiated and signed the Korean Armistice Agreement on July 27, 1953, that finally led to a "complete cessation of all hostilities in Korea." Though he had secured the agreement with the threat of employing the United States' unparalleled nuclear weaponry, he openly was loath to use it. Instead, Eisenhower preferred to promote peace, saying, "Every gun that is made, every warship launched, every rocket fired, signifies in the final sense a theft from those who hunger and are not fed, those who are cold and are not clothed."

Eisenhower then turned his focus on strengthening NATO and establishing the Southeast Asia Treaty Organization (SEATO) to combat communist expansion in that region. And after sending troops to Lebanon to end the Muslim insurrection against the pro-Western government in July 1958, he never sent armed forces again into active duty throughout his presidency, although he did not hesitate to authorize defense spending.

Still, Eisenhower worried about the spread of communism, and he authorized the Central Intelligence Agency to undertake covert operations against its influence around the world, two of which led to toppling the governments of Iran in 1953 and Guatemala in 1954.

Simultaneously, Eisenhower built the Atoms for Peace program, which stressed the use of atomic and nuclear power for peaceful endeavors rather than war and warned of potential unholy alliances between big business and the military. He also presided over the integration of Washington, D.C., and pushed through the Civil Rights Act of 1957 that compelled the desegregation of Little Rock, Arkansas' Central High School.

By 1957, Eisenhower had also turned his attention to the heavens when he authorized the creation of the National Aeronautical and Space Agency (NASA) in an effort to stay ahead of the Soviets in the space race.

Despite all of this, Ohio University history professor Chester J. Pach Jr. points out that "Although he avoided war, Eisenhower did not achieve the peace he desired. He hoped for détente with the Soviet Union but instead left to his successor an intensified Cold War." And his support for the pro-Western government in South Vietnam paved the way for future U.S. involvement in the Vietnam War.

1953–1961

BORN OCT. 14, 1890, DENISON, TEXAS
DIED MARCH 28, 1969, WASHINGTON, D.C.
BURIAL SITE ABILENE, KANSAS
EDUCATION U.S. MILITARY ACADEMY, WEST POINT
POLITICAL PARTY REPUBLICAN
AGE AT INAUGURATION 62
VICE PRESIDENT RICHARD M. NIXON
OPPONENT ADLAI STEVENSON (1ST AND 2ND TERMS)
OCCUPATIONS BEFORE PRESIDENCY SOLDIER; PRESIDENT OF COLUMBIA UNIVERSITY
OTHER OFFICES NONE
FIRST LADY MARIE "MAMIE" GENEVA DOUD EISENHOWER
NICKNAME IKE

Clockwise from top left: With Allied military commanders in England in the spring of 1944; celebrating his election victory with his wife, Mamie, in 1952; pushing through desegregation in Little Rock, Arkansas, in 1957; getting NASA off the ground in 1958.

JOHN FITZGERALD
KENNEDY

DESPITE SOLID DOMESTIC POLICIES, JFK'S INTERNATIONAL ENTANGLEMENTS AND UNTIMELY DEATH LEFT MYSTERIES STILL HOVERING OVER HIS PRESIDENCY

★ ★ ☆

RANKING
11

THE MOST ENDURING MYSTERY OF JOHN F. KENNEDY'S legacy is whether or not Lee Harvey Oswald acted alone in assassinating him. But for historians, a close second is, as president, would Kennedy have withdrawn U.S. forces stationed in Vietnam or escalated the war?

Kennedy was one of nine children born into a privileged Massachusetts political family, and as a boy he suffered from numerous ailments, worrying his parents that he wouldn't survive. He went on to graduate from Harvard before joining the Navy, where his ship, the *PT-109*, was sunk in 1943 by a Japanese warship, and he heroically rescued several members of his crew. Upon returning home, Jack decided to go into politics, serving three terms in Congress before being elected senator and then deciding to run for president.

Young, handsome and charismatic, with a glamorous wife and young children, Kennedy was elected after defeating Richard Nixon in a close race, making him the nation's first Catholic president, and its youngest elected, at age 43. He brought a new generation into power and

> **KEY ACHIEVEMENTS**
> • Supported the space program and challenged the nation to land a man on the moon by the end of the 1960s.
> • Resolved the Cuban Missile Crisis during tense negotiations with Soviet leader Nikita Khrushchev.
> • Banned segregation in federally funded housing.

recognized the need for all Americans to engage in their communities to help the country succeed. "Ask not what your country can do for you, ask what you can do for your country," he said in his inauguration speech.

Domestically, Kennedy fulfilled his promise of optimistic leadership by creating the Peace Corps and kicking off Project Apollo, which would eventually lead to the first manned moon landing in 1969. He also abolished the federal death penalty and made strides in civil rights by signing executive orders prohibiting segregation and committed to a civil rights bill before he died (it was eventually passed by his successor, Lyndon Johnson).

But in foreign affairs, Kennedy was put to the test right from his inauguration, running headfirst into the Cold War, beginning with the failed Bay of Pigs invasion—an attempt to remove Fidel Castro from power in Cuba—in April 1961, and continuing with the Berlin Crisis in June 1961 (which led to the Soviets building the Berlin Wall) and the Cuban missile crisis in October 1962. Kennedy and his mostly young, inexperienced policy team managed

DID YOU KNOW?

Kennedy is the only U.S. president to be awarded the Pulitzer Prize, winning in 1957 for his book *Profiles in Courage*.

Kennedy was one of the wealthiest presidents to take office, and he donated his full salary to charity.

ALL THE PRESIDENT'S VEHICLES

POTUS GETS FREE RIDES IN VERY FANCY CARS (AND PLANES AND HELICOPTERS)

AIR FORCE ONE

The term "Air Force One" originated in 1953 during President Dwight D. Eisenhower's tenure. When the Air Force delivered a Boeing jet designated Special Air Mission (SAM) 26000 to John F. Kennedy, he, acting on his wife Jacqueline's advice, hired famed industrial designer Raymond Loewy to help select the color scheme and lettering for Air Force One—a design that continues to this day. The SAM 26000 flew from 1962 to 1998, serving presidents from Kennedy to Bill Clinton.

MARINE ONE

Marine One is the call sign of any United States Marine Corps aircraft carrying the POTUS. Eisenhower was the first to use a helicopter for transport and it was during his presidency when the White House's South Lawn was cleared to become a landing zone for Marine One helicopters. At an inauguration, Marines transport outgoing presidents for one last ride from the Capitol to Andrews Joint Base in Prince George's County, Maryland.

THE BEAST

The most well-known automobile associated with the presidency is the open-top Lincoln Continental that JFK was riding in that fateful day in Dallas. Since his assassination, presidents continued to use the Lincoln Continental until President Ronald Reagan switched to a Cadillac outfitted with bulletproof glass. It was during President Barack Obama's tenure that the Beast was introduced. The custom Cadillac weighs 10 tons and is built to withstand a biological attack, with 8-inch-thick walls and 5-inch-thick bulletproof windows.

the latter two crises deftly, including averting nuclear war with Russia over the Cuba blockade. In July 1963, Kennedy succeeded in persuading Nikita Khrushchev to sign a nuclear test ban treaty.

Vietnam was different. Kennedy first pursued a path to work with South Vietnam's president and longtime U.S. ally Ngo Dinh Diem, dispatching Vice President Lyndon B. Johnson in May 1961 to increase the U.S. commitment to helping defeat communism in the region. JFK's administration provided approximately $40 million in military and logistical aid, and began sending special advisers to train South Vietnamese soldiers to beat back Viet Cong insurgents. The threat continued to intensify, however, and when JFK sent envoys in October 1961 to assess the situation, they recommended sending 8,000 troops. Kennedy opted to commit fewer.

The following year, the Kennedy administration pursued new tactics in South Vietnam, including the U.S. Air Force dumping Agent Orange and other chemicals from planes to defoliate the jungles that Viet Cong forces used for engaging in guerrilla warfare. These strategies failed to deter the Viet Cong, and the use of Agent Orange eventually came back to haunt the U.S., when its own soldiers, and many Vietnamese, reported illnesses associated with the chemicals, including cancer. The fighting with the Viet Cong also began to take a greater toll. Casualties of American soldiers grew to 109 by 1962, compared to 14 a year earlier.

Kennedy's backing of Diem continued into 1963, though U.S. support of his regime was becoming tenuous. By April, Kennedy sounded dismayed. "We don't have a prayer of staying in Vietnam," he said. "Those people hate us. They are going to throw our asses out of there at any point. But I can't give up that territory to the Communists and get the American people to reelect me."

The U.S. continued to ramp up support of South Vietnamese troops, but the Viet Cong forces fought above their weight. In August,

The presidential motorcade, moments before the assassination

the new U.S. ambassador, Henry Cabot Lodge, a seasoned diplomat who had been a foe of Kennedy, traveled to Vietnam just as Diem had begun a ruthless crackdown against Buddhist monks using CIA-trained South Vietnamese troops. Lodge was tasked with convincing Diem and his adviser-brother Ngo Dinh Nhu to step down, and for them both to voluntarily leave the country. They refused, and Washington sent Cable 243, dated August 24, 1963, instructing Diem to remove Nhu from his government. Again, Diem refused, and Lodge advised working with South Vietnamese generals to support a coup.

In early September, Kennedy discussed Vietnam during two televised interviews, one with Walter Cronkite on CBS and another with David Brinkley and Chet Huntley on NBC. In the latter interview, Kennedy addressed the idea that American influence had its limitations in

"A MAN MAY DIE, NATIONS MAY RISE AND FALL, BUT AN IDEA LIVES ON."

JOHN F. KENNEDY

Vietnam, saying, "We can't make everyone in our image, and there are a good many people who don't want to go in our image."

In October, intelligence reports suggested that Vietnamese General Duong Van Minh wanted to gauge how the U.S. would react to a coup. Kennedy told Lodge to assist clandestinely, though without approving Diem's assassination. On November 2, 1963, South Vietnamese forces led by Minh arrested Diem and Nhu and executed the brothers. At the time, the U.S. had an estimated 16,000 military advisers in the country.

Just three weeks later, on November 22, 1963, Kennedy was assassinated. His death stunned and rocked the nation and spurred numerous conspiracy theories that Lee Harvey Oswald, who was arrested for the crime, had not, in fact, acted alone—the conclusion of the Warren Commission set to investigate the killing. Despite theories that organized crime may have had a hand in Kennedy's death, none to date have been proven.

But the question as to how Kennedy would have handled the post-Diem era in Vietnam also lingers. Kennedy's boyhood friend and longtime supporter, McGeorge Bundy, who was made special assistant for national security affairs in the Kennedy administration, went on to become one of the architects of escalating the war under President Johnson. However, Secretary of Defense Robert McNamara, who would commission the painstakingly detailed Vietnam Study Task Force

in 1967 (later leaked and known as the Pentagon Papers) had been a Diem supporter. McNamara would later insinuate in his 1995 book *In Retrospect* that Kennedy had planned a withdrawal of U.S. troops—though this assertion was ridiculed in reviews. Historian Noam Chomsky wrote, "Two weeks before Kennedy's assassination, there is not a phrase in the voluminous internal record that even hints at withdrawal without victory."

Despite the mysteries that Kennedy's assassination left behind, his presidency has been largely gauged as a success, albeit one of unfulfilled promises. Shortly after his death, his widow, Jacqueline, invited a journalist from *Life* magazine to the Kennedy compound in Hyannis Port, Massachusetts. There, she took steps to ensure her husband's near-mythic legacy in office by quoting from the popular musical, *Camelot*, that gave his time in office its nickname: "Don't let it be forgot, that once there was a spot, for one brief, shining moment that was known as Camelot. There'll be great presidents again...but there will never be another Camelot."

1961–1963

BORN MAY 29, 1917, BROOKLINE, MASSACHUSETTS
DIED NOV. 22, 1963, DALLAS, TEXAS
BURIAL SITE ARLINGTON NATIONAL CEMETERY, ARLINGTON, VIRGINIA
EDUCATION HARVARD UNIVERSITY
POLITICAL PARTY DEMOCRATIC
AGE AT INAUGURATION 43
VICE PRESIDENT LYNDON B. JOHNSON
OPPONENT RICHARD M. NIXON
OCCUPATIONS BEFORE PRESIDENCY AUTHOR, POLITICIAN, MILITARY OFFICER, JOURNALIST
OTHER OFFICES MEMBER OF U.S. HOUSE OF REPRESENTATIVES; MEMBER OF U.S. SENATE
FIRST LADY JACQUELINE LEE BOUVIER KENNEDY
NICKNAMES JFK, JACK

Clockwise from top left: Offering hope at his inauguration address in 1961; the 1969 moon landing got its start with Kennedy's Project Apollo; discussing strategy with Secretary of Defense Robert McNamara (center); Vietnam casualties begin to mount.

LYNDON BAINES
JOHNSON

TAKING OVER AFTER JFK'S ASSASSINATION, LBJ FOUND HIS PRESIDENCY UPENDED BY VIETNAM

★ ★ ☆

RANKING
10

HAD IT NOT BEEN FOR THE HORROR OF AN INHERITED WAR in Vietnam he could not figure out how to win, Lyndon B. Johnson would have been regarded as one of the greatest presidents in American history.

"Under Johnson's domestic leadership, Republicans and Democrats worked together to engineer the greatest advancements in civil rights since the Civil War," said noted presidential historian Doris Kearns Goodwin. "Yet, as the terrain shifted from the domestic policies of the Great Society to the war in Vietnam, Johnson demonstrated an epic failure of leadership that would compromise his credibility, forever scar his legacy, and nearly tear the country apart."

Johnson assumed the role of commander in chief under the worst conditions. He was sworn into office hours after President John F. Kennedy was assassinated in Dallas on November 22, 1963, and in front of JFK's widow, Jacqueline, who was still covered in blood from the shocking shooting.

"Those first few days," Johnson remembered, "Vietnam was on top of the agenda, before the visiting heads of state even got home from the funeral." The new president was never convinced the war could be won. He even told national security adviser McGeorge Bundy, "I don't think it's worth fighting for and I don't think we can get out. And it's just the biggest damn mess."

If Johnson had chosen not to go fully into war, he would be fondly remembered for the string of accomplishments of his Great Society program, which led to groundbreaking legislation creating Medicare and Medicaid, guaranteeing health care for seniors and the poor. He also expanded Social Security and made the food stamps program permanent. LBJ also established the Job Corps, created a federal work-study program and initiated the Head Start program to provide early education for disadvantaged students. It was also Johnson who established the 1963 Clean Air Act to fight pollution (a policy Nixon would build on) and the Wilderness Act, which protected millions of acres of American wilderness.

KEY ACHIEVEMENTS

- Created Medicare and Medicaid.

- Signed the Civil Rights Act, outlawing discrimination based on race or color, sex, religion or national origin.

- Signed the Voting Rights Act, securing votes for minorities.

DID YOU KNOW?
Johnson is one of only four people (John Tyler, Andrew Johnson and Richard Nixon are the others) to have been a U.S. representative, Senate Majority Leader, vice president and president.

Johnson began his career as a teacher at a small school near the Mexican border, but entered politics in 1931.

"POVERTY MUST NOT BE A BAR TO LEARNING, AND LEARNING MUST OFFER AN ESCAPE FROM POVERTY."

LYNDON B. JOHNSON

His sweeping civil reforms led to his winning the 1964 election over hard-line conservative Arizona Sen. Barry Goldwater in a historically lopsided landslide.

Johnson's Civil Rights Act that year was the most expansive of its kind to that point. It prohibited discrimination on the basis of race, color, religion, sex or national origin, banned segregation and provided for the integration of schools and other public facilities. It also weakened his support from Southern Democrats and, combined with the specter of the quagmire that was the Vietnam War, led to the end of his presidency.

Despite his promises to not escalate the Vietnam conflict that had begun under Dwight Eisenhower and ramped up under Kennedy, Johnson increased the number of troops from 16,000 when he took office to more than 500,000 by the end of his term in 1968. He refused to show weakness in the face of adversity. LBJ believed Eisenhower "sat on his fanny" and allowed Cuba to be overrun by Fidel Castro's Communist insurgents in 1959. He wasn't about to let the same thing happen in Vietnam.

Despite the unparalleled escalation of troops and airstrikes, no headway was made and the war dragged, on with American casualties mounting.

More than 30,000 American soldiers were left dead in the jungles of Vietnam by 1968.

The president who had enjoyed an unprecedented 80 percent approval rating in 1963 saw that number plummet to an equally shocking low of 26 percent by 1967. Johnson's popularity hit rock bottom with American anti-war protestors chanting, "Hey, hey, LBJ, how many kids did you kill today?" When it became obvious that he would face strong opposition from his own party in the 1968 election, a dejected Johnson announced he would not seek reelection. "I shall not seek, nor will I accept, the nomination of my party for another term as your president," he said on March 31, 1968, explaining he wanted to focus on the peace process and his domestic reforms without being distracted by another campaign.

Unfortunately, the war in Vietnam continued until 1975, and Johnson's legacy would forever be defined by it—to the point where his vast accomplishments remain sadly underrated.

1963–1969

BORN AUG. 27, 1908, STONEWALL, GILLESPIE COUNTY, TEXAS
DIED JAN. 22, 1973, JOHNSON CITY, TEXAS
BURIAL SITE LBJ RANCH, JOHNSON CITY, TEXAS
EDUCATION GEORGETOWN LAW SCHOOL
POLITICAL PARTY DEMOCRATIC
AGE AT INAUGURATION 55
VICE PRESIDENT HUBERT H. HUMPHREY
OPPONENT BARRY M. GOLDWATER
OCCUPATIONS BEFORE PRESIDENCY TEACHER, RANCHER, POLITICIAN
OTHER OFFICES DIRECTOR, NATIONAL YOUTH ADMINISTRATION DIRECTOR; MEMBER OF U.S. HOUSE OF REPRESENTATIVES; MEMBER OF U.S. SENATE; U.S. VICE PRESIDENT
FIRST LADY CLAUDIA ALTA "LADY BIRD" TAYLOR JOHNSON
NICKNAME LBJ

Clockwise from top left: Johnson was sworn in hours after Kennedy's assassination, next to Jackie Kennedy; signing the Civil Rights Act in 1964; listening to taped messages about the fighting in Vietnam; the war's death toll dragged down the presidency.

RICHARD MILHOUS
NIXON

LIKE HIS PREDECESSOR, NIXON'S LEGACY IN VIETNAM WOULD BE ONE OF FAILURE

★ ★ ★

RANKING
33

RICHARD M. NIXON WAS ELECTED BECAUSE HE PROMISED Americans that he would end Lyndon Johnson's unwanted war "with honor" and leave a democratic government in South Vietnam that preserved our interests in Southeast Asia. He technically kept that promise, but Nixon's legacy will always be defined by the dark Watergate scandal that led him to be the only president ever forced to resign his position as commander in chief.

During his first term in office, however, the now largely reviled Republican spearheaded admirable progressive domestic reforms in welfare, heath care, civil rights, energy and environmental policies. Still, he initially focused on ending the war, and five days after assuming office on January 20, 1969, Nixon dispatched a team of negotiators to Paris to meet with representatives of North and South Vietnam. The results were disastrous: The North Vietnamese refused to accept anything less than the surrender of the South and Nixon vowed, "I'm not going to be the first American president to lose a war!"

But that's exactly what would eventually happen. In his desperation to quash the North, which had launched a furious battle, Nixon responded secretly, and illegally dropped 4 million tons of explosives on neighboring Cambodia to cut the supply lines to the North Vietnamese Army. He also stepped up the ground war, as U.S. and South Vietnamese forces pursued a policy of "maximum pressure" against North Vietnamese and Viet Cong allies in the South.

His tactics wrought furious criticism from anti-war protesting students and political opponents. "I feel it is both senseless and irresponsible to continue to send our young men to their deaths to capture hills and positions that have no relation to ending this conflict," Sen. Edward Kennedy said of the "Hamburger Hill" debacle that left 72 American soldiers dead.

Realizing there was no easy way out, Nixon appeared on television on November 3, 1969, to plead for the patience of his middle-class base as he struggled to end the war. "So tonight, to you, the great 'silent majority' of my fellow Americans, I ask for your support," Nixon said. "Let us be united for peace. Let us also be united against defeat."

Beyond Vietnam, Nixon introduced a historic foreign policy plan that called for the U.S. to

KEY ACHIEVEMENTS
• Reopened relations with The People's Republic of China.
• Gained praise for "saving" Israel during the 1973 Yom Kippur War.
• Founded the Environmental Protection Agency.

DID YOU KNOW?
When Nixon took office, he had his Secret Service detail wear white double-breasted tunics and hats. This didn't last, and the uniforms were donated to a high school marching band.

An outstanding law student, Nixon graduated third in his class from Duke University.

THE DIPLOMAT
Nixon failed with Vietnam, but established stronger ties to both Israel and Egypt.

Nixon announces the U.S. invasion of Cambodia on May 30, 1970.

On a visit to the People's Republic of China, Nixon made diplomatic breakthroughs.

strengthen all existing treaty commitments with its allies. As a result, he established stronger ties to both Israel and Egypt, eliminating Soviet diplomatic dominance in the region.

When not focused on concerns abroad, Nixon turned to domestic matters, where he enjoyed greater success. He founded the Environmental Protection Agency in 1970, resulting in what would now be considered "green initiatives" with the Clean Air Act, Clean Water Act and the Mammal Marine Protection Act. And as much as he was loathed by the vast majority of American youth—especially after the shooting of anti-war protesting students at Kent State University in 1970—Nixon supported the Constitutional amendment lowering the voting age to 18.

Still, Vietnam remained his main concern, and Nixon knew the war would impact his reelection. During the lead-up to the election, Nixon dominated in the polls, fueled by the string of foreign and domestic accomplishments from his first term of

office, and the impending withdrawal of American troops from Vietnam that National Security Adviser Henry Kissinger was secretly pursuing.

Republicans were excited about the possibility of facing ultra-liberal Democratic candidate Sen. George McGovern (whom Nixon would later defeat in a landslide election). But on June 17, 1972, Nixon's paranoia provided a green light for a needless break-in of Democratic National Headquarters, lighting the fuse for explosive charges that would forever tarnish what may have been considered one of the most successful administrations in history.

As the Watergate scandal percolated in the papers, the U.S. and the Democratic Republic of Vietnam signed a peace agreement in January 1973, with Nixon assuring South Vietnamese President Nguyen Van Thieu that America would protect his country against further invasion. But with domestic opposition and the impeachment that would force Nixon to resign 19 months later, those promises were never kept.

After the agreement, Nixon took advantage of what he called the "peace dividend" to finance social welfare services and enforce civil rights through the Equal Employment Opportunity Commission. He initiated affirmative action, reduced segregation in public schools, and reserved jobs in federally funded construction projects for minorities. He helped all American laborers by creating the Occupational Safety and Health Administration, which provided for safer conditions. While the Senate didn't pass Nixon's Family Assistance Program (FAP), which would have provided working and nonworking poor families with a guaranteed annual income, support for the concept would lead to similar programs such as Supplemental Security Income, providing a guaranteed income to the elderly, the blind and the disabled; and automatic cost-of-living adjustments for Social Security recipients. He also introduced a Federal revenue-sharing

"NO EVENT IN AMERICAN HISTORY IS MORE MISUNDERSTOOD THAN THE VIETNAM WAR."

RICHARD NIXON

program, providing state and local governments with billions of federal tax dollars.

Even his many deserved detractors grudgingly credit Richard Nixon for his groundbreaking foreign policy achievements. Most point to his historic opening of diplomatic relations with the People's Republic of China, when he became the first American president to set foot in the totalitarian Communist country in 1972.

That same year, President Nixon participated in the Strategic Arms Limitation Talks (SALT) with Soviet Secretary General Leonid Brezhnev as part of an effort to temper the Cold War through a diplomatic détente. As a result, the two former enemies signed the Anti-Ballistic Missile (ABM) Treaty, helping to calm U.S.-Soviet tensions by cooling the looming threat of nuclear escalation by either of the world's two superpowers. And during the 1973 Yom Kippur War, Nixon supported Israel with massive aid, which Prime Minister Golda Meir later said saved her country.

Yet despite his stunning accomplishments, Nixon will be remembered for the second-rate burglary and bungled cover-up that exposed his paranoia-fueled shortcomings. During impeachment proceedings in July 1974, secret tapes that the courts had ordered Nixon to turn over revealed his attempts to derail FBI investigations, an enemies list targeted for IRS harassment, hush money payouts and the president's own humiliating racial prejudices. Nixon was impeached by the end of the month and he resigned his position as commander in chief on August 9, 1974.

1969-1974

BORN JAN. 9, 1913, YORBA LINDA, CALIFORNIA
DIED APRIL 22, 1994, NEW YORK CITY, NEW YORK
BURIAL SITE RICHARD NIXON LIBRARY, YORBA LINDA, CALIFORNIA
EDUCATION WHITTIER COLLEGE, DUKE UNIVERSITY LAW
POLITICAL PARTY REPUBLICAN
AGE AT INAUGURATION 56
VICE PRESIDENTS SPIRO AGNEW (1ST TERM); GERALD FORD (2ND TERM)
OPPONENTS HUBERT HUMPHREY (1ST TERM); GEORGE McGOVERN (2ND TERM)
OCCUPATIONS BEFORE PRESIDENCY LAWYER, BUSINESSMAN, PUBLIC OFFICIAL
OTHER OFFICES MEMBER OF THE U.S. HOUSE OF REPRESENTATIVES; MEMBER OF THE SENATE; U.S. VICE PRESIDENT
FIRST LADY THELMA "PAT" CATHERINE RYAN
NICKNAME TRICKY DICK

GERALD R.
FORD

DEALT A TERRIBLE HAND, FORD GAMBLED
WHEN HE PARDONED NIXON

★ ★ ★

IN THE 244-YEAR HISTORY OF THE UNITED STATES, ONLY one man has served as both vice president and president without receiving one electoral vote.

On December 6, 1973, under the 25th Amendment, Gerald Ford was appointed the 40th vice president after Spiro Agnew resigned for pleading no contest to felony tax evasion. As Republican minority leader in the House, Ford was well-respected and his confirmation proved that: He was confirmed in the Senate by a vote of 92-3, and in the House 387-35.

Almost exactly eight months later, Ford was sworn in as the 38th president after President Richard Nixon resigned in the wake of the Watergate scandal. Ford, having no connection to the scandal, willingly took control of the country at a time of unrivaled turbulence, saying in his inaugural address: "I am acutely aware that you have not elected me as your president by your ballots, and so I ask you to confirm me as your president with your prayers."

And while he went on to say, "My fellow Americans, our long national nightmare is over," it wasn't. Nixon was out of office but still faced a number of charges, and he would certainly have to stand trial—until Ford granted him a "full, free, and absolute pardon...for all offenses against the United States." Meant to bring the nation together, it only stirred the controversy up even more, and Ford saw his approval rating plummet from 71 percent upon taking over the presidency down to 50 percent after the pardon, and it later dropped to 40 percent.

Ford's pardon of Nixon weighed heavily on his two-and-a-half-year presidency, as did the conclusion of the Vietnam War, which officially ended in April 1975. The economy was suffocating, with inflation rising as high as 12.3 percent. Ford tried to alleviate some of the pressure on the country with policies such as clemency for draft dodgers, and WIN (Whip Inflation Now). And when the Cambodian Khmer Rouge forces seized the *SS Mayaguez* and held the American crew hostage in May 1975, Ford ordered military action to rescue the crew. But despite a bump in his approval rating, his bid for reelection was dashed by Georgia Democrat Jimmy Carter, who addressed Ford at the start of his inauguration speech, saying, "For myself and for our nation, I want to thank my predecessor for all he has done to heal our land."

KEY ACHIEVEMENTS

• Signed the Federal Elections Campaign Act, the first bill to reform campaign financing since the 1920s.

• Signed Helsinki Accords with all European nations to improve relations with the Soviet Union.

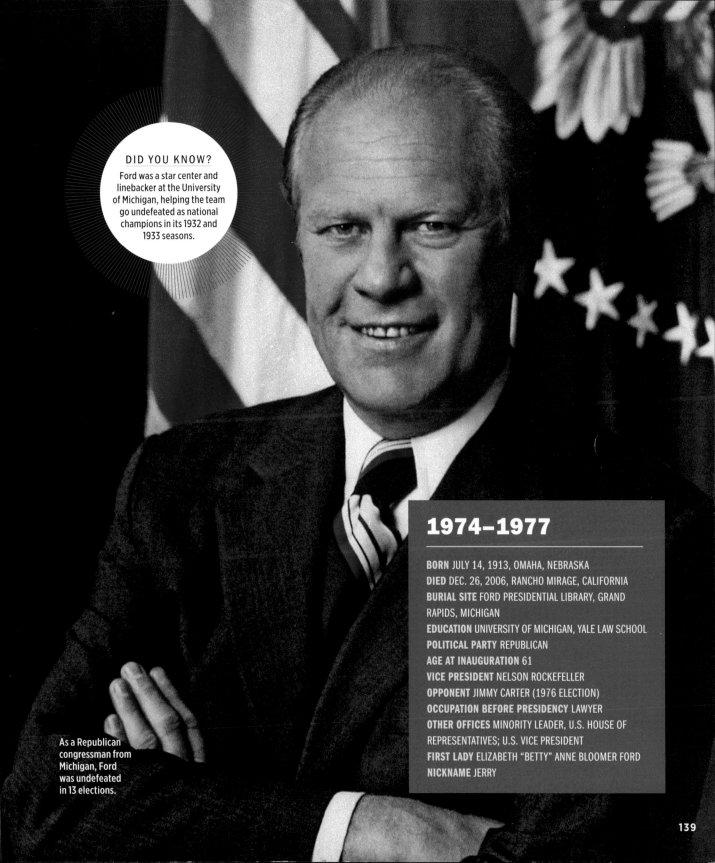

DID YOU KNOW?
Ford was a star center and linebacker at the University of Michigan, helping the team go undefeated as national champions in its 1932 and 1933 seasons.

1974–1977

BORN JULY 14, 1913, OMAHA, NEBRASKA
DIED DEC. 26, 2006, RANCHO MIRAGE, CALIFORNIA
BURIAL SITE FORD PRESIDENTIAL LIBRARY, GRAND RAPIDS, MICHIGAN
EDUCATION UNIVERSITY OF MICHIGAN, YALE LAW SCHOOL
POLITICAL PARTY REPUBLICAN
AGE AT INAUGURATION 61
VICE PRESIDENT NELSON ROCKEFELLER
OPPONENT JIMMY CARTER (1976 ELECTION)
OCCUPATION BEFORE PRESIDENCY LAWYER
OTHER OFFICES MINORITY LEADER, U.S. HOUSE OF REPRESENTATIVES; U.S. VICE PRESIDENT
FIRST LADY ELIZABETH "BETTY" ANNE BLOOMER FORD
NICKNAME JERRY

As a Republican congressman from Michigan, Ford was undefeated in 13 elections.

JAMES EARL
CARTER

HE ALWAYS LOOKED OUT FOR OTHERS,
BUT THEN CAME THE IRAN HOSTAGE CRISIS

★ ★ ★

RANKING
26

ON THE NATIONAL LEVEL, JIMMY CARTER, A FORMER peanut farm tycoon, was considered a Washington outsider. As an outspoken Georgia governor with roots in the deep South, Carter worked tirelessly to revoke laws that challenged the civil rights of blacks to vote. His presidential campaign was grounded in his support for human rights and in his inaugural address he articulated his view: "Because we are free, we can never be indifferent to the fate of freedom elsewhere. Our moral sense dictates a clear-cut preference for those societies which share with us an abiding respect for individual human rights."

While president, Carter's foreign policy focused on creating and strengthening infrastructures in his administration that applied human-rights considerations to both military and economic aid to foreign countries.

Carter also focused on setting up talks between Israel's Prime Minister Menachem Begin and Egypt's President Anwar Sadat at Camp David, which were held on September 5, 1978. Twelve days later the Camp David Accords were signed,

KEY ACHIEVEMENTS

• Mediated negotiations between Israeli Prime Minister Menachem Begin and Egyptian President Anwar Sadat that resulted in the Camp David Accords.

• Established the Department of Energy and Department of Education.

a peace treaty between the two nations that had been at war without any reduction in intensity for more than a decade. The treaty called for Israel to return the Sinai Peninsula, land the country conquered during the Yom Kippur War in 1973, and for Egypt to extend full diplomatic recognition of Israel. Begin and Sadat won the Nobel Peace Price for these efforts. Robert A. Strong, professor of politics at Washington and Lee University, says the Camp David Accords are often considered to be the most significant foreign policy achievement of Carter's administration.

It was, however, an Iranian foreign policy crisis that tested the Carter administration and became his lasting legacy. Carter had announced his candidacy for reelection in February 1979. He probably should have waited: In July 1979, a group of revolutionaries inspired by Ayatollah Ruhollah Khomeini forced the American- and British-backed Shah Mohammad Reza Pahlavi, whose pro-Western ideology protected the oil interests of both countries, to flee Iran for Egypt. Carter did not initially defend the deposed shah, whose human rights record was

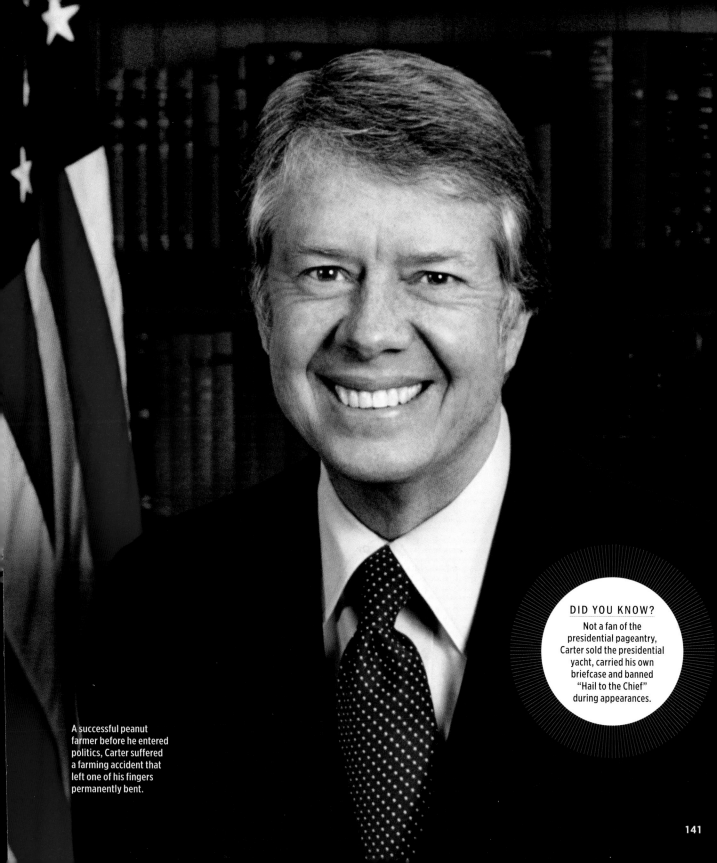

DID YOU KNOW?
Not a fan of the
presidential pageantry,
Carter sold the presidential
yacht, carried his own
briefcase and banned
"Hail to the Chief"
during appearances.

A successful peanut
farmer before he entered
politics, Carter suffered
a farming accident that
left one of his fingers
permanently bent.

"AMERICA DID NOT INVENT HUMAN RIGHTS. IN A VERY REAL SENSE...HUMAN RIGHTS INVENTED AMERICA."

JIMMY CARTER

brutal, but after learning of his lymphatic cancer, he allowed him entry into the United States for medical treatment as a humanitarian gesture. Explaining the motivation years later, Carter said, "I was told that New York had the only medical facility that was capable of possibly saving his life and was reminded that the Iranian officials had promised to protect our people in Iran. When all the circumstances were described to me, I agreed."

Carter's move was a political catastrophe. In response, on November 4, 1979, Iranian students charged the American embassy in Tehran and seized 66 American diplomats and citizens—holding 52 of them hostage for more than a year. Peter L. Hahn, professor of history and dean of arts and humanities at The Ohio State University, states, "Carter blundered because of vacillation, shortsighted thinking, a disregard for identified risk and inept implementation that included zero precautions to protect against disaster."

The students terrorized the hostages, and Carter launched Operation Eagle Claw in April 1980, sending in the Army's Delta Force in an attempt to rescue them. But everything went wrong. The operation cost the lives of eight American servicemen who were killed when their helicopter crashed and the operation was terminated.

While the hostage crisis was going on, Carter also had to deal with the Soviet Union's two-month invasion of Afghanistan. This led to Carter withdrawing from the Strategic Arms Limitation Talks treaty (SALT II) with the Soviet Union, an agreement he originally signed in June 1979. SALT II was aimed at curbing nuclear weapons deployment by the world's rival superpowers. Carter also placed an embargo on grain sales to the Soviet Union—and the U.S., along with numerous other countries, wound up boycotting the 1980 Summer Olympics in Moscow.

The 1980 election, meanwhile, was dominated by a news cycle that focused on the hostage crisis and the ineffectual negotiating and rescue operation undertaken by Carter. He was defeated in a landslide by Republican Ronald Reagan, earning only 49 electoral votes to Reagan's 489. The hostages were released, after 444 days in captivity, just hours after Reagan was sworn in.

Despite the problems in his flawed presidency, however, Carter has been recognized for his work since he left the White House. In 2002, he won the Nobel Peace Prize "for his decades of untiring effort to find peaceful solutions to international conflicts, to advance democracy and human rights, and to promote economic and social development."

1977-1981

BORN OCT. 1, 1924, PLAINS, GEORGIA
EDUCATION UNION COLLEGE
POLITICAL PARTY DEMOCRATIC
AGE AT INAUGURATION 53
VICE PRESIDENT WALTER F. MONDALE
OPPONENT GERALD FORD
OCCUPATIONS BEFORE PRESIDENCY SOLDIER, FARMER, WAREHOUSEMAN
OTHER OFFICES GOVERNOR OF GEORGIA; STATE LEGISLATIVE SERVICE, GEORGIA
FIRST LADY ELEANOR ROSALYNN SMITH CARTER
NICKNAME JIMMY

Clockwise from top left: Carter made history with Anwar Sadat and Menachem Begin at the Camp David Accords; he was awarded the Nobel Peace Prize in 2002 for his decades of service; his treatment of the Shah of Iran angered Iranians; the subsequent Iran hostage crisis undermined his presidency.

RONALD WILSON
REAGAN

THE POPULAR POLITICIAN HAD AN UNUSUAL PATH TO THE OVAL OFFICE AND, SOME SAY, A RECORD OF EXAGGERATED ACCOMPLISHMENTS

★ ★ ★

RANKING
12

RONALD REAGAN IS PERHAPS OUR MOST MYTHOLOGIZED president. He was, without a doubt, one of the most successful, and certainly one of the most beloved, leaving office with a 55 percent approval rating, matched in history only by Franklin D. Roosevelt and Bill Clinton.

Reagan changed the way government was perceived and actually operated. He came to Washington determined to extract it from daily lives as much as possible, to cut and simplify taxes and to deregulate business, which he did to what some say was an ultimately unhealthy degree. A former union head, he defeated the Professional Air Traffic Controllers Organization (PATCO) in an ugly and dangerous fight, but he handled it superbly and, history shows, he was correct to do so, stating the strike was a "peril to national safety."

He expanded the military and introduced the then science fiction-y concept of creating what was to be a space shield over the U.S., nicknamed Star Wars but officially known as the Strategic Defense Initiative (SDI). Its objective was to be able to shoot down Soviet

KEY ACHIEVEMENTS

• Economic policies lowered unemployment and inflation.

• Reagonomics led to an economic boom and GDP growth.

• Defeating the PATCO strike in 1981 led to a massive drop in illegal work stoppages against the government.

• Met with Mikhail Gorbachev and signed the Intermediate Range Nuclear Forces Treaty.

nuclear missiles from outer space with lasers. Although that project never came to be, versions of the plans morphed throughout succeeding presidencies and today we have a network of land-based anti-ballistic missile defenses that follow the same principle. But just the notion that the U.S. was developing such a system was incredibly effective in precipitating the end of the Cold War, as the Russians virtually bankrupted themselves trying to keep up with America's technological warfare advances. ("Why can't we just lean on the Soviets until they go broke?" Reagan once joked to his top aides.)

He also appointed the first woman to the Supreme Court, Sandra Day O'Connor.

Reagan was known as the Great Communicator, but on some issues he was often incredibly tone-deaf. For years, he ignored the AIDS crisis decimating gay communities across America—almost 30,000 people had died of the syndrome before he first publicly mentioned the epidemic. He was loathed by AIDS activists and gay people, and by liberals in general, who saw him as a

DID YOU KNOW?
Reagan was partially deaf in one ear due to an accident on a movie set, when a gun went off next to his head.

Growing up during the Depression, Reagan idolized FDR and would imitate his fireside chats.

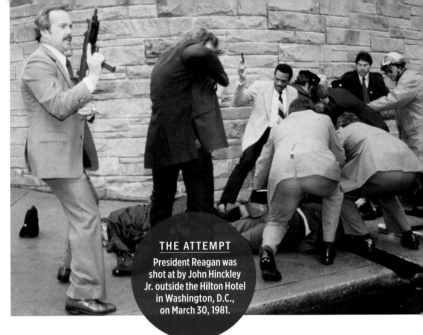

THE ATTEMPT
President Reagan was shot at by John Hinckley Jr. outside the Hilton Hotel in Washington, D.C., on March 30, 1981.

IN THE LINE OF FIRE

MOST ASSASSINATION ATTEMPTS WERE HOPELESS, AND SOME WOULD-BE ASSASSINS LITERALLY COULDN'T SHOOT STRAIGHT

There have been an awful lot of attempts to assassinate our country's presidents—16 of the 45 have had attacks on their lives—and four were successful. Maybe five.

The first attempt on a president's life was against Andrew Jackson in 1835, when assailant Richard Lawrence's gun misfired twice at close range. Lawrence was soon arrested and declared insane. Franklin D. Roosevelt was shot at and missed five times by Giuseppe Zangara in 1933. Gerald Ford came across two potential killers in the space of three weeks. First, Charles Manson follower Lynette "Squeaky" Fromme's gun jammed as she pulled the trigger at point-blank range in early September 1975; later that month, Sara Jane Moore outright missed from close up because a disabled veteran next to her grabbed her arm when he saw the gun. Fromme and Moore are the only two women to openly attempt to kill a president.

Ronald Reagan was shot by John Hinckley Jr., but survived and famously told his wife, Nancy, "I forgot to duck." Theodore Roosevelt was also shot, in 1912 after he had left office, and thundered with even more machismo: "It takes more than that to kill a Bull Moose!" True to his word, he died of a heart attack in 1919 with the bullet still in him.

Abraham Lincoln had the most attempts made against him: seven. The first six included an intended knifing in Baltimore; plots to send him clothing infected with yellow fever and smallpox; plans to blow up the White House; and two missed shootings. The seventh attempt, sadly, didn't fail, when John Wilkes Booth shot him in the head at Ford's Theatre.

Lincoln was the first U.S. president to be assassinated, and two more were killed in the next 36 years: James Garfield in July 1881 and William McKinley in September 1901. The fourth president who was assassinated—John F. Kennedy—was shot in Dallas in November 1963, and a number of coincidences between his and Lincoln's murder were noted. For one, both men's vice presidents and successors were Johnsons (Andrew and Lyndon); they had been elected to their first term in Congress 100 years apart (Lincoln in 1846; Kennedy in 1946). Similarly, they were elected president in 1860 and 1960, respectively. Both of their assassins were killed before being brought to justice. And Kennedy's secretary was surnamed Lincoln.

Anyone who knows their presidential history knows that Warren Harding was also assassinated. Or was he? Officially, he died of a massive heart attack at the Palace Hotel in San Francisco in 1923. Almost immediately, suspicions arose that his wife, Florence, who refused to allow an autopsy, poisoned him after learning he'd been unfaithful to her. A private detective hired by Florence to discover the infidelity, later wrote a book, *The Strange Death of President Harding*, in which he claimed she did.

The detective, Gaston Means, was a convicted criminal before he became a detective, so there's an asterisk to his credibility, and the doctors who examined Harding's corpse concluded his death was from heart failure. Few of Harding's papers remain: His widow destroyed almost all of them, personal and official, in the month following his death.

regressive president and feared (wrongly, it turned out) that he would undo the safety nets progressively championed by many of his predecessors.

And in response to complaints about the deterioration of school lunches and the diminished nutrition in children's diets, he famously claimed ketchup was a vegetable.

He was staunchly conservative and his time in office most significantly nurtured and encouraged the rise of the Christian Right as a political force, which on the local level did unravel a lot of social progress, particularly in regard to a woman's right to an abortion. And the Christian Right remains, more than 30 years after he left office, a powerful influence on national politics. It's ironic that the man who, while campaigning, once poetically and inspiringly promised to "restore the great, confident roar of American progress and growth and optimism," was responsible for allowing the greatest intrusion of repressive religious agendas into society since the Pilgrims arrived in the 1600s.

Reagan was born, raised and schooled in various towns across northern Illinois, the state of another outsize Republican president—Abraham Lincoln. He played football, acted in school plays and in 1937, at the age of 26, while working as a play-by-play announcer for the Chicago Cubs for a small-town Iowa radio station, traveled to California to cover some games. While in Los Angeles, he landed—and passed—a screen test for Warner Bros. movies, and Hollywood had a new leading man.

There he made 50 movies, most famously 1940's *Knute Rockne, All American*, in which he played Notre Dame football player George Gipp and uttered the immortal line, "Win one for the Gipper." Perhaps most infamously, he also played Professor Peter Boyd—and second fiddle to a chimp—in 1951's *Bedtime for Bonzo*, no one's finest hour. Reagan once said of the mostly B-movies he made that the studio "didn't want them good, they wanted them Thursday." (When he was president, he good-naturedly screened *Bedtime for Bonzo* for staff and guests at Camp David.)

He was elected governor of California in 1966, beating Democratic incumbent Pat Brown (father of Jerry Brown, who succeeded Reagan in 1975). Reagan served two terms, with an ideological fervor that propelled him to the national stage. In 1968, he made his first attempt for the Republican nomination, losing out to Richard Nixon. He tried again, unsuccessfully, in 1976, when incumbent Gerald Ford, having become president when Nixon resigned, beat Reagan by the smallest of margins. Ford eventually lost to Jimmy Carter in the general election. In 1980, Reagan did win the nomination and went on to defeat Carter, who was dragged down by the continuing Iran hostage crisis. Reagan won the Electoral College by an astonishing 10 to 1 ratio—489 votes to 49. (He was, at 69 years old, the oldest man ever elected president at the time.) When he ran for reelection

By co-starring with a chimp, Reagan gave political opponents (and comedians) plenty of fodder in future years.

"ALL GREAT CHANGE IN AMERICA BEGINS AT THE DINNER TABLE."

RONALD REAGAN

four years later, he did even better, beating the hapless Walter Mondale 525 to 13, winning 49 out of 50 states.

During his presidency, Reagan, pursuing his policies that became known as Reaganomics, successfully turned the economy around, reducing inflation from 12.5 percent to 4.4 percent, a staggering accomplishment. He also increased the GDP at an average annual growth rate of 3.4 percent. He rode out the potentially presidency-ending Iran-Contra scandal, in which it was exposed that his administration covertly supplied arms to Communist-fighting rebel groups in Central America, in defiance of Congress—which had passed a law forbidding exactly that. He befriended Soviet President Mikhail Gorbachev and together they created the immensely important missile-reduction treaty that ultimately made the world safer. His unprecedented outreach to Gorbachev tremendously reduced the inflamed tensions between the two nuclear superpowers.

Reagan presided over the beginning of the end of the Cold War, but he is erroneously credited with personally bringing down the Berlin Wall, the symbolic surrender of the Soviets. As president in 1987 he had stood next to the wall on the West German side, and dramatically called upon Gorbachev to "tear down this wall." But when it was physically opened two years later, during George H.W. Bush's presidency, it was actually an accident. An East German border officer misunderstood

a command about the lifting of travel visas and ordered crossing points of the wall opened, allowing East Germans to pour through into West Berlin. Reagan did weaken the Soviets by sucking them into an economic arms race, but it was Gorbachev who, realizing the Soviet empire couldn't be sustained, put into motion the dynamics that dissolved it, and opened the Eastern Bloc.

By the time Ronald Reagan left office, the country was in a far better place than when he came in. It was not as utopian as his most fervent acolytes like to think, but also not as dreary as his most passionate detractors claim.

Author Peter Schrag said Reagan's "sunny personality" was important. "His [sometimes excessive] self-confidence and his folksy ability to reach Middle Americans seemed to insulate him from the fallout of the policy disasters and embarrassments and the effects of the neglect and mismanagement that so often plagued the White House." Reagan was an imperfect man, but he was a great man. We'll always take that.

1981–1989

BORN FEB. 6, 1911, TAMPICO, ILLINOIS
DIED JUNE 5, 2004, LOS ANGELES
BURIAL SITE RONALD REAGAN PRESIDENTIAL LIBRARY, SIMI VALLEY, CALIFORNIA
EDUCATION EUREKA COLLEGE
POLITICAL PARTY REPUBLICAN
AGE AT INAUGURATION 69
VICE PRESIDENT GEORGE H.W. BUSH
OPPONENTS JIMMY CARTER (1ST TERM); WALTER MONDALE (2ND TERM)
OCCUPATIONS BEFORE PRESIDENCY MILITARY, RADIO ANNOUNCER, ACTOR
OTHER OFFICE GOVERNOR OF CALIFORNIA
FIRST LADY NANCY DAVIS REAGAN
NICKNAMES THE GREAT COMMUNICATOR, DUTCH, RONNIE RAYGUN, THE TEFLON PRESIDENT

Clockwise from top left: Reagan playing football growing up in Illinois; in 1940, portraying Notre Dame legend George Gipp in *Knute Rockne, All American*; thawing Soviet relationships with Mikhail Gorbachev; at the Berlin Wall before it fell.

GEORGE H. W.
BUSH

A YEAR AFTER ANNOUNCING THE COLD WAR WAS OVER,
HE LIBERATED KUWAIT IN THE GULF WAR

★ ★ ☆

RANKING
24

THOUGH HIS SON WOULD LAY CLAIM TO THE PHRASE "compassionate conservatism," George H.W. Bush rode into office on a pledge to uphold American values and make the United States a "kinder and gentler nation," as he said in his inaugural address.

Coming from a family dedicated to public service—his father was a U.S. senator from Connecticut—Bush became one of the Navy's youngest-ever pilots when he received his wings at 19. He served in World War II and received the Distinguished Flying Cross for bravery after his plane was shot down in the Pacific.

After a career in the oil industry, which took him to Texas, and working in a series of political appointments, including as director of the CIA, he drew on his history of civil service as Ronald Reagan's vice president, and made an impact at the 1988 Republican Convention when he secured the nomination for president, giving a memorable speech in which he pledged not to raise taxes with a phrase that would come back to haunt him: "Read my lips. No new taxes." It was a promise he wasn't able to keep when the economy slipped into a mild recession.

KEY ACHIEVEMENTS
- Raised the minimum wage.
- Met with Soviet President Mikhail Gorbachev and announced the Cold War was over.
- Signed the Americans With Disabilities Act, the Clean Air Act and the Immigration Act.

In office, Bush's domestic efforts included encouraging volunteerism, which he often referred to as "a thousand points of light," and he signed the Americans with Disabilities Act. Following 1989's catastrophic Exxon Valdez oil spill, he signed the Oil Pollution Act that would work to avoid future spills. With two seats opening on the Supreme Court during his tenure, Bush appointed David Souter to replace liberal William Brennan, and then Clarence Thomas to fill the seat of legendary liberal Thurgood Marshall. Opposition to Thomas during his confirmation hearings, however, increased when Anita Hill came forward to testify that Thomas had sexually harassed her when they worked together at the Equal Employment Opportunity Commission. Still, Thomas was narrowly confirmed and has become one of the most conservative judges of his era.

In foreign affairs, Bush worked with German Chancellor Helmut Kohl to aid the reunification of Germany after the fall of the Berlin Wall and signed the Strategic Arms Reduction Treaty (START I) with Soviet President Mikhail Gorbachev, which pledged a 30 percent cut in nuclear weapons by both nations.

DID YOU KNOW?
Bush flew 58 combat missions for the Navy during World War II and was awarded three Air Medals, as well as the Distinguished Flying Cross.

For his 75th, 80th, 85th and 90th birthdays, Bush celebrated by going skydiving.

THE PERSIAN GULF WAR, EXPLAINED

The origins of the 1991 Persian Gulf War conflict began when the Iraqi army annexed Kuwait following accusations by Iraq's president, Saddam Hussein, that the Kuwaitis were stealing oil from fields along the two countries' border. Hussein also accused Kuwait and Saudi Arabia of conspiring to keep oil prices artificially low to appease Western allies. Shortly after sending his troops into Kuwait, Hussein announced that it had become the "19th province" of Iraq. The move gave Iraq control of 20 percent of the world's oil production.

The United Nations soon imposed sanctions on Iraq, and Saudi Arabia's King Fahd met with U.S. Secretary of Defense Dick Cheney, reportedly requesting military assistance. The U.S. began sending Air Force fighter jets to Saudi Arabia, and President Bush, British Prime Minister Margaret Thatcher and others assembled a coalition, amassing troops on the border between Saudi Arabia, Iraq and Kuwait.

Americans overwhelmingly backed the idea of sending troops to Saudi Arabia, and opposed military action to oust Iraq from Kuwait. But the Bush administration's talk about needing "a new world order" sparked controversy in foreign policy circles.

In his address to announce the launch of Operation Desert Storm, President Bush carefully explained that the U.S., the United Nations, Middle Eastern nations and others had tried to negotiate with Hussein since Iraqi troops rolled into neighboring Kuwait, but sanctions and diplomatic discussions had failed to sway the dictator to pull back troops. Additionally, the president said, the Iraqi army had behaved barbarically during its occupation, raping, plundering and killing.

During the speech, Bush also suggested that the operation would wipe out Hussein's chemical weapons stockpile and thwart its nuclear capabilities, invoking the idea that the Iraqis had been developing a "weapon of mass destruction"—a term that has since become associated with his son, President George W. Bush, and the 2003 coalition invasion of Iraq that eventually toppled Hussein.

About 1,000 sorties were flown in the first 24 hours of Desert Storm, and Americans watched the action on cable news networks. The massive air and naval offense quickly overpowered Iraqi troops with air assaults that featured new technology such as laser-guided "smart bombs" and cruise missiles. In response, Hussein launched SCUD missiles at military targets inside Saudi Arabia and Israel, but they were no match for the U.S. and its allies. By March 1991, the brief war was over.

BUSH ON THE GROUND

The president and Gen. Norman Schwarzkopf visited Saudi Arabia during Operation Desert Shield

But President Bush's greatest challenge would come from the Middle East. On the night of January 16, 1991, he appeared in a live televised address to announced the commencement of Operation Desert Storm, where U.S.–led coalition forces had begun retaliating against Saddam Hussein and Iraq over its invasion of Kuwait in what became known as the Persian Gulf War.

That previous November, the United Nations had passed a resolution authorizing the removal of Iraq from Kuwait "by all means necessary." For several months, the Bush administration had been arguing that a "new world order" was needed, in which United Nations peacekeepers could play an important role in resolving conflicts like the annexation of Kuwait. The administration also asserted that removing Iraqi troops from Kuwait was necessary to prevent Hussein from pursuing development of nuclear weapons and attempting to imperialize the Middle East and control its oil fields.

"WE KNOW WHAT WORKS. FREEDOM WORKS. WE KNOW WHAT'S RIGHT. FREEDOM IS RIGHT."

GEORGE H.W. BUSH

1989–1993

BORN JUNE 12, 1924, MILTON, MASSACHUSETTS
DIED NOV. 30, 2018, HOUSTON, TEXAS
BURIAL SITE GEORGE H.W. BUSH PRESIDENTIAL LIBRARY AND MUSEUM, COLLEGE STATION, TEXAS
EDUCATION YALE UNIVERSITY
POLITICAL PARTY REPUBLICAN
AGE AT INAUGURATION 64
VICE PRESIDENT DAN QUAYLE
OPPONENT MICHAEL DUKAKIS
OCCUPATIONS BEFORE PRESIDENCY MILITARY OFFICER, BUSINESSMAN
OTHER OFFICES MEMBER OF THE U.S. HOUSE OF REPRESENTATIVES; AMBASSADOR TO THE UNITED NATIONS; CHAIRMAN, REPUBLICAN NATIONAL COMMITTEE; UNITED STATES ENVOY TO CHINA; DIRECTOR, CENTRAL INTELLIGENCE AGENCY; VICE PRESIDENT
FIRST LADY BARBARA PIERCE BUSH
NICKNAME POPPY

By the time President Bush gave his televised address, Congress and the American public had gotten behind the idea of retaliation against Hussein. The president reassured the public during his speech and proclaimed full support of the troops while asserting that this would not be "another Vietnam." He declared: "We will not fail."

In a few short weeks, following a massive naval and air offense, Iraq's troops appeared routed. The U.S.-led forces launched a ground assault on February 24, 1991, and in one day, effectively finished the war, as Iraqi soldiers surrendered to coalition troops en masse. Coalition forces liberated Kuwait and pushed across the border into Iraq, but stopped short of advancing on Baghdad and toppling Hussein. On February 28, President Bush declared a ceasefire, officially ending the war. Hussein accepted terms on April 6, 1991, and remained in power until the 2003 invasion of Iraq.

But Bush wasn't able to withstand the political battle he faced at home for reelection. With conservatives angry over his tax increases and Texas billionaire Ross Perot muddying the waters while running as an independent, Arkansas Gov. Bill Clinton claimed the Democratic nomination and won the presidency in November 1992. Though he was defeated, some historians consider George H. W. Bush as having the most successful one-term presidency in our history.

WILLIAM JEFFERSON
CLINTON

*HE TOOTED HIS OWN HORN
TO CONNECT WITH YOUNG AMERICANS*

★ ★ ★

**RANKING
18**

ON JANUARY 20, 1993, WILLIAM JEFFERSON CLINTON, Arkansas' second-youngest governor, became the third-youngest president—after Theodore Roosevelt and Kennedy—to hold the office. In his inauguration address, Clinton opened with majestic words of hope, saying, "This ceremony is held in the depth of winter, but by the words we speak and the faces we show the world, we force the spring, a spring reborn in the world's oldest democracy that brings forth the vision and courage to reinvent America."

That message of change had been a constant in Clinton's run-up to the presidency. In a bold departure from serious sit-downs with political journalists and mainstream media, the then-45-year-old governor of Arkansas and Democratic presidential hopeful had appeared live on *The Arsenio Hall Show* on June 3, 1992, wearing a pair of Ray-Ban Wayfarer sunglasses and a bright yellow tie. Channeling one of the Blue Brothers, Clinton whaled on his saxophone for a rousing rendition of Elvis Presley's "Heartbreak

KEY ACHIEVEMENTS

- Created more than 22 million jobs in less than eight years.
- Lowest unemployment rate in 30 years.
- Signed the Brady Bill, leading to more than 600,000 prohibited persons being stopped from buying guns. Gun crime declined 40 percent.
- Deactivated more than 1,700 nuclear warheads, 300 launchers and 425 land- and submarine-based missiles from the former Soviet Union.

Hotel," followed by Billie Holiday's "God Bless The Child." Afterward, he sat with Hall for one of his most memorable interviews. Clinton, who was referred to by Republicans in 1992 as a "failed governor of a small Southern state," said years later that appearance was "one of the more substantive interviews I've done." And with the blare of his horn, Bill Clinton had become a household name.

It was a turn of events that the young boy, born in Hope, Arkansas three months after his father had died in a car accident, might not have foreseen. Although perhaps it was not entirely surprising: By the time he was in high school and met President John F. Kennedy while a delegate to Boys Nation, Clinton's interest in politics and public service had been sparked.

Clinton rose through the ranks of Arkansas politics to become governor in 1983. For the 1992 presidential election, he brought on 44-year-old Al Gore as his running mate, and the two relative youngsters signaled a change coming in American political leadership.

DID YOU KNOW?
In 1996, Clinton became the first Democrat to be elected to a second term since FDR in 1936.

Clinton has won two Grammys: One for Best Spoken Word Album (2005) and one for Best Spoken Word Album for Children (2004).

A 16-year-old Clinton shook his idol JFK's hand at a gathering in Washington, D.C., in 1963.

DID YOU KNOW?
Clinton, here with Arsenio Hall, played sax as a teen in a band called Three Blind Mice.

Clinton's appearance on Arsenio Hall's show had been the brainchild of Clinton media adviser Mandy Grunwald, who recognized that "it was the end of one way of communicating with voters and the beginning of another. They just didn't know that yet." This new era of communicating with young, urban voters through pop culture landed a powerful blow to the campaign of independent candidate Ross Perot and threatened the incumbent, President George H.W. Bush. There was no denying that Bush's prudent slogan, "A Proud Tradition"—when pitted against Clinton's more idealistic "It's Time to Change America"—was in trouble.

Once he was elected, more changes echoed throughout Clinton's first term, and he devoted vast energy to health care reform. Just five days after his inauguration, he enlisted first lady Hillary Rodham Clinton, an accomplished lawyer and advocate for children, to head the Task Force on National Health Care Reform. The proposed bill was supposed to fix a "badly broken" system. Under this bill, every citizen would have a "health care security card," giving them "universal coverage" for high-quality health care and to choose their physician, as well as to control the skyrocketing costs of health care. This ambitious plan was met with deep criticism from conservatives and the health-service industry. The bill was eventually defeated, although he did sign the Family Medical Leave Act, a bill that requires companies to provide their employees with up

"IF YOU LIVE LONG ENOUGH, YOU'LL MAKE MISTAKES, BUT IF YOU LEARN FROM THEM, YOU'LL BE A BETTER PERSON."

BILL CLINTON

to three months of unpaid leave for family and medical emergencies. And in August 1996, Clinton did expand health care coverage, allowing workers who change or lose their jobs to keep their health insurance coverage.

Clinton's first term marked huge economic growth, which enabled more families to buy homes. The homeownership rate increased from 64.2 percent in 1992 to 67.7 percent, the highest rate ever. And in 1993, Clinton created the National Service Program, making it possible for students to repay federal student loans through community service.

In 1996, Clinton's reelection campaign was invigorated by the successes of his first term, most notably the preservation of Medicare and welfare programs, and the strong economy and fiscal discipline of his administration (he would go on to sign the country's first balanced budget in three decades in 1998). But his popularity took a hit after he first lied about and then acknowledged an inappropriate relationship with a young intern, Monica Lewinsky. For this character defect and moral failure, Clinton was eventually impeached for sexual misconduct on December 19, 1998, and later acquitted, on February 12, 1999—but not before 400 historians signed a letter objecting to the proceedings, declaring that they "deplore the

present drive to impeach" Clinton, amid the fear that it would have "the most serious implications for our constitutional order."

"More attention could have been paid to the tangible ways that American lives were made better during those eight years," historian Ted Widmer wrote in the *Observer*, "in ways ranging from education to crime prevention, job creation and conservation. It wasn't always the sexiest news, but it was happening every day."

"In the end," history professor David Greenberg wrote in *Washington Monthly*, "Clinton did much more than survive. He made the Democratic Party viable again in presidential elections. He reoriented liberalism, retaining its core commitments to a mixed economy, a welfare state, civil rights, civil liberties, and an internationalist foreign policy—while also acknowledging where its past policies on welfare, crime, and other issues had lost the confidence of the American people."

After leaving office in 2001 with one of the highest approval ratings of any president since World War II, Clinton emerged with his image, and his saxophone, intact.

1993–2001

BORN AUG. 19, 1946, HOPE, ARKANSAS
EDUCATION GEORGETOWN UNIVERSITY, OXFORD UNIVERSITY, YALE UNIVERSITY LAW SCHOOL
POLITICAL PARTY DEMOCRATIC
AGE AT INAUGURATION 47
VICE PRESIDENT AL GORE
OPPONENTS GEORGE H.W. BUSH (1ST TERM), ROBERT DOLE (2ND TERM)
OCCUPATIONS BEFORE PRESIDENCY PROFESSOR, LAWYER
OTHER OFFICES ATTORNEY GENERAL OF ARKANSAS; GOVERNOR OF ARKANSAS
FIRST LADY HILLARY RODHAM CLINTON
NICKNAMES SLICK WILLIE, BUBBA

Clockwise from top left: Giving his 1993 inauguration speech; focusing on health care legislation with wife, Hillary; endorsing his veep, Al Gore, for the presidency in August 2000; greeting Monica Lewinsky at a fundraiser in October 1996.

159

GEORGE W.
BUSH

A TERRORIST ATTACK, WARS IN AFGHANISTAN AND IRAQ,
AND A CATASTROPHIC HURRICANE SHAPED HIS TWO TERMS

★ ★ ★

RANKING
32

SEVEN MONTHS AFTER HE WAS INAUGURATED FOLLOWING one of the most controversial general elections ever (remember hanging chads and Florida recounts?), George W. Bush was faced with a controversial moral decision when legislation about stem cell research reached his desk.

It was thought that stem cells harvested from discarded human embryos could offer drastic advances in medicine, including potential cures for Parkinson's disease and other degenerative disorders. Bush's thought process, although well-calculated (he summoned scientists to the Oval Office and had in-depth discussions with religious leaders, including Pope John Paul II) was shaped by "deeply held beliefs," and he stated, "This issue forces us to confront fundamental questions about the beginnings of life and the ends of science." The bill was supposed to be one of the biggest markers during his young presidency; he announced on August 9, 2001, that he would restrict federal funds, making them only available for research on existing stem cell lines, not for further destruction of human embryos.

KEY ACHIEVEMENTS

• Signed a $1.35 trillion tax cut into law, slashing income tax rates across the board and providing for the gradual elimination of the estate tax.

• Overhauled Medicare, the biggest expansion of an entitlement program since Johnson's Great Society. The bill included the program's first prescription drug benefits and created incentives for private insurance companies to cover Medicare subscribers.

Thirty-three days later, on September 11, the U.S. was attacked by al-Qaida when two hijacked planes crashed into the World Trade Center in New York City, another crashed in Pennsylvania and a fourth into the Pentagon, making the latter the first time Washington, D.C., had been attacked since the War of 1812. Combined, it was the largest loss of life from a foreign attack on American soil. While speaking to a classroom of students at Emma E. Booker Elementary School in Sarasota, Florida, White House Chief of Staff Andrew Card, who initially thought the first plane crash into the Twin Towers was an accident, whispered into the president's right ear, "A second plane hit the second tower. America is under attack."

That night, the president appeared on TV. "Today, our nation saw evil— the very worst of human nature— and we responded with the best of America." In his memoir *Decision Points*, Bush said, "My blood was boiling. We were going to find out who did this, and kick their ass."

Bush declared war on terror. The PATRIOT Act was passed one month later, allowing government

DID YOU KNOW?
Bush is just the fourth Republican president to be elected and serve two full terms (the others are Grant, Eisenhower and Reagan).

A lifelong baseball fan, Bush was part owner of the Texas Rangers, buying a 2 percent stake for $800,000 and later selling it for $14.9 million.

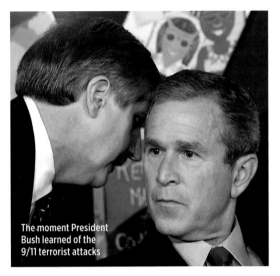

The moment President Bush learned of the 9/11 terrorist attacks

agencies more liberties with regards to citizens' privacy. The Department of Homeland Security was established. The controversial Terrorist Surveillance Program was enacted in secret, carefully designed to protect the civil liberties of innocent U.S. citizens while opening the door for monitoring al-Qaeda operatives who might be living in the U.S.

Bush had a 90 percent approval rating after his first year in office, a point higher than his father's at the end of the Gulf War in 1991. But the remainder of his first term would be marred with a declaration of war against Iraq while on a quest to find weapons of mass destruction based on incorrect intelligence reports.

"The war in Iraq was a biblical struggle of good versus evil," wrote biographer Jean Edward Smith.

BILOXI BLUES

Bush visited Biloxi, Mississippi, during his tour of the Gulf Coast in the aftermath of Hurricane Katrina.

"His decision to bring democracy to Iraq was equally arbitrary and unilateral."

But despite growing tensions stateside with wars in Iraq and Afghanistan, Bush won reelection in 2004, receiving 62,040,610 votes, the most in the history of presidential elections at that time.

In 2005, during Bush's second term, the Gulf Coast was ravaged by Hurricane Katrina, causing $161 billion in damages, the costliest natural disaster in American history. The Mississippi coastline was decimated by the storm's 125 mph winds, while 80 percent of New Orleans, home to more than 450,000 people, was flooded.

Four days after Katrina made landfall, Bush met with Democratic Gov. Kathleen Blanco and New Orleans Mayor Ray Nagin. No one seemed to know who was in charge of providing security and relief supplies to the city and local leaders were in no rush to give the keys to the federal government. Former New Orleans Homeland Security Director Col. Terry Ebbert said, "FEMA has been here for three days, yet there is no command and control. We can send massive amounts of aid to tsunami victims but we can't bail out the city of New Orleans."

"USE POWER TO HELP PEOPLE."

GEORGE W. BUSH

Moved by the tragedy, Bush, who called himself a "compassionate conservative," deployed 7,000 active duty troops to New Orleans, but did not grant them law enforcement powers. Even FEMA's director, Michael Brown, was forced to resign for his lack of leadership during the crisis.

Bush also pushed for immigration reform and border security during his second term. But the Comprehensive Immigration Reform Act of 2007, which was supposed to give legal status to an estimated 12 million undocumented immigrants from Latin America and create a merit-based system for future immigrants along with a temporary work program, exposed an absence of support from Bush's own Republican Party, who fiercely opposed the bill.

"The failure of immigration reform points out larger concerns about the direction of our politics," said Bush about Congress blocking free trade agreements with Colombia, Panama and South Korea. "I recognize the genuine anxiety that people feel about foreign competition. But our economy, our security and our culture would all be weakened by an attempt to wall ourselves off from the world."

Mexican President Felipe Calderon said the Senate had made a "great mistake" in rejecting the bill. "The U.S. economy cannot keep going without migrant labor," he said.

The bill was Bush's last chance at getting a piece of major domestic legislation passed. The failed legislation, Katrina and the ongoing wars in Iraq and Afghanistan took a toll on his reputation. Democrats regained control of Congress in 2006 and his approval rating sunk to 34 percent. As his second term came to an end, the country saw its largest economic recession since World War II.

2001–2009

BORN JULY 6, 1946, NEW HAVEN, CONNECTICUT
EDUCATION YALE UNIVERSITY, HARVARD BUSINESS SCHOOL
POLITICAL PARTY REPUBLICAN
AGE AT INAUGURATION 54
VICE PRESIDENT DICK CHENEY
OPPONENTS AL GORE (1ST TERM), JOHN KERRY (2ND TERM)
OCCUPATIONS BEFORE PRESIDENCY BOARD MEMBER, TOM BROWN, INC.; FOUNDER, CEO OF BUSH EXPLORATION; GENERAL PARTNER, TEXAS RANGERS
OTHER OFFICE GOVERNOR OF TEXAS
FIRST LADY LAURA WELCH BUSH
NICKNAMES DUBYA, W., SHRUB

BARACK HUSSEIN
OBAMA

*A NUMBER OF "FIRSTS" DEFINED
HIS TRAILBLAZING PRESIDENCY*

★ ★ ★

**RANKING
9**

THE FIRST AFRICAN AMERICAN TO BECOME PRESIDENT, Barack Hussein Obama became a groundbreaking commander in chief in more ways than one. During his eight years in office, Obama was the first president to appoint a former first lady (Hillary Clinton) to his Cabinet; to endorse same-sex marriage; and to visit a federal prison, a mosque and a synagogue. He passed groundbreaking health care reform, with mixed results. But perhaps his most significant achievement was helping to rescue an economy that was teetering on the edge of catastrophe as he came into office.

Born to a Kenyan father and a mother from Kansas, Obama was raised in Hawaii and graduated from Columbia University and Harvard Law School before moving to Chicago and serving in the Illinois State Senate. In 2004, while still a senatorial candidate (having won the Illinois primary in a landslide), he delivered the keynote address at the Democratic National Convention, where he made an impact by insisting, "There is not a liberal America and a conservative America—there is the United States of America. There is not a Black America and a White America and Latino America and Asian America—there's the United States of America."

While that speech set him up as a potential front-runner for the 2008 election, his success wasn't assured, as he faced off against Hillary Clinton in the primaries and eventually against Senator John McCain in the general election. But his embrace of social media helped him reach a whole new generation of voters. And in a speech on the eve of the New Hampshire primary, he set the tone for his campaign by proclaiming he would usher in an era of change. "We will remember that there is something happening in America, that we are not as divided as our politics suggest, that we are one people, we are one nation," he said. "And, together, we will begin the next great chapter in the American story, with three words that will ring from coast to coast, from sea to shining sea: Yes, we can." Eleven months later, he won the White House with nearly 53 percent of the vote.

KEY ACHIEVEMENTS

• Provided health coverage to millions via the Affordable Care Act.

• Assassinated terrorist Osama bin Laden.

• Ended the 2008 recession with the $800 billion American Recovery and Reinvestment Act.

• Brokered a nuclear peace agreement with Iran.

DID YOU KNOW?
Obama was the first African American editor of the *Harvard Law Review*.

Obama goes by the code name "Renegade" to the Secret Service agents who protect him.

OUR FIRST "SOCIAL" PRESIDENT MADE EVERYTHING LOOK COOL

For President Obama, looking cool was his natural disposition. His poise in times of crisis made you feel protected. And the advent of social media and the growing strength of the internet allowed for him to show everyone it was OK for the most powerful person in the world to share his true self with the entire planet.

During his 2008 campaign, with a reported 100 people running his digital presence, Obama took to Twitter to show off his tech savvy. And while the technology as we know it today was not around for his predecessors, he followed in the footsteps of those who utilized the latest innovations to advance their presence. John F. Kennedy, for one, is credited for being the first president to master the medium of television, while Franklin D. Roosevelt used the radio to communicate with the country during his "fireside chats" in the 1930s and '40s.

The Obama administration understood the blanket approach of getting the word out. Upon Obama's 2009 inauguration, the White House embraced social media, joining Facebook, Flickr, iTunes, Twitter, Vimeo, even MySpace. First lady Michelle Obama posted her

He got laughs during the 2007 election campaign by appearing on *SNL*.

Backing up Jimmy Fallon on *The Tonight Show* made Obama feel relatable.

first photo on Instagram in 2013. Two years later, the president tweeted for the first time from the newly created @POTUS account. In 2017, Snapchat was used to promote the president's State of the Union address.

Obama, whom *The Atlantic* described as being "inseparable" from his Blackberry, put social media's full use to great effect. This influx of networking sites allowed the self-described "geek" to welcome his followers (and doubters) into his life, making his world a much smaller place.

Moreover, on social media, Obama was comfortable being whomever you wanted him to be: fun, loving, suave, talented, the cool dad. During his first presidential campaign, he appeared on *Saturday Night Live* in the Halloween 2007 episode as himself, wearing a mask of himself. He slow-jammed the news on *The Tonight Show Starring Jimmy Fallon*. Many of his posts and appearances went viral, including one memorable post that showed just how personable and human Obama was: A young boy named Jacob visited the White House and asked the president, "I want to know if my hair is just like yours," to which Obama responded, "Why don't you touch it and see for yourself," bending down so Jacob could feel his hair. Jacob did and said, "Yes, it does feel the same."

THE SITUATION
Obama and his staff watched the raid on Osama bin Laden unfold in real time in the Situation Room.

In 2009, as Obama took the oath of office, the Dow Jones was at 6,000 and unemployment was at nearly 8 percent. His administration introduced a stimulus package that gave vast relief to banks and investment firms and helped right the sinking American auto industry.

The ambitious American Recovery and Reinvestment Act, which was 50 percent bigger than the New Deal in terms of dollars allotted, helped improve the nation's overall infrastructure. These efforts paid off: On Obama's departure from the presidency in 2017, the Dow Jones was just off

the 20,000 mark and unemployment had sunk to 4.8 percent.

Writing in *The New York Times*, Paul Krugman called Obama "an extremely consequential president, doing more to advance the progressive agenda than anyone since L.B.J." However, not everything his administration tackled yielded satisfactory results.

Undeniably his most important piece of legislation, the Affordable Care Act (aka Obamacare) has contributed to medical coverage for millions of Americans previously without

"IF YOU'RE WALKING DOWN THE RIGHT PATH AND YOU'RE WILLING TO KEEP WALKING, EVENTUALLY YOU'LL MAKE PROGRESS."

BARACK OBAMA

it, while prohibiting insurance companies from denying coverage due to preexisting conditions. But it's also his most disputed legislation.

Krugman and others have taken issue with other achievements of his, which, Krugman wrote, "have depended at every stage on accepting half loaves as being better than none: health reform that leaves the system largely private; financial reform that seriously restricts Wall Street's abuses without fully breaking its power; higher taxes on the rich but no full-scale assault on inequality."

Still, the so-called Dodd-Frank reforms, passed in the wake of the financial meltdown of 2008, provided useful restrictions on risky behavior by Wall Street investors. He also signed the repeal of "Don't ask, don't tell," which allowed gay men and lesbians to serve openly in the military, and became the first president to support gay marriage. Add to that a number of important steps to protect the environment, including the establishment of new rules governing offshore drilling and the coal industry's contribution to global warming—a new Environmental Protection Agency regulation would require the nation's coal-powered plants to reduce emissions by 32 percent

from their 2005 levels by 2030. In addition, he issued executive orders that addressed important issues related to immigration and gun control.

On the global front, Obama was awarded the Nobel Peace Prize in 2009 for his efforts at strengthening international diplomacy. He ended the U.S. involvement in Iraq undertaken by George W. Bush, and approved the covert operation that resulted in the killing of Osama bin Laden, the mastermind of the 9/11 attacks. Obama also pledged the support of the U.S. in signing the Paris Agreement, a commitment by 197 nations to lower carbon emissions, in November 2015. Two months later, he led six nations in negotiating a deal in which Iran agreed to end its nuclear weapons program. Another two months after that, he became the first sitting president since 1928 to visit Cuba, opening the door for U.S. citizens to freely visit the country.

As historian Julian Zelizer notes in *The Presidency of Barack Obama: A First Historical Assessment*, Obama "turned out to be a very effective policymaker but not a tremendously successful party builder," battling an extremely oppositional Republican Party while trying to bring the country together.

2009–2017

BORN AUG. 4, 1961, HONOLULU, HAWAII
EDUCATION COLUMBIA UNIVERSITY, HARVARD LAW SCHOOL
POLITICAL PARTY DEMOCRATIC
AGE AT INAUGURATION 48
VICE PRESIDENT JOE BIDEN
OPPONENTS JOHN McCAIN (1ST TERM); MITT ROMNEY (2ND TERM)
OCCUPATIONS BEFORE PRESIDENCY LAWYER, POLITICIAN
OTHER OFFICES MEMBER OF U.S. SENATE; MEMBER OF ILLINOIS STATE SENATE
FIRST LADY MICHELLE ROBINSON OBAMA
NICKNAME BARRY

Clockwise from top left: As senator, celebrating the publication of his best-selling book; signing the Affordable Care Act in 2010; the White House commemmorates the legalization of same-sex marriage; with members of his cabinet (including Secretary of State Hillary Clinton).

DONALD JOHN
TRUMP

TRUMP RESHAPED THE PRESIDENCY IN HIS OWN IMAGE

★ ★ ☆ ──────────────────────

RANKING
TBD

IN FRONT OF AN ENTHUSIASTIC CROWD, MANY OF THEM wearing their trademark MAGA (Make America Great Again) hats, Chief Justice John G. Roberts Jr. administered the presidential oath of office to Donald John Trump on January 20, 2017. In his address, businessman turned politician Trump called himself the protector of the "forgotten men and women" in America. He promised them: "[You] will be forgotten no longer. Everyone is listening to you now. At the center of this movement is a crucial conviction: that a nation exists to serve its citizens. Americans want great schools for their children, safe neighborhoods for their families, and good jobs for themselves."

Defying pundits who predicted a Hillary Clinton victory, Trump entered the White House in an enviable position, with a Republican majority in both the House and the Senate. He made the most of it.

Born and raised in Queens, New York, the son of a real estate developer, Trump went to college at the Wharton School of the University of Pennsylvania before following in his father's footsteps—and then surpassing him to become a billionaire real estate tycoon. His Trump Organization expanded to include projects outside of New York City—in Atlantic City, Florida and internationally—and he became a household name after producer Mark Burnett helped turn Trump into a reality TV star on *The Apprentice*. But politics had never been far from his interests.

Once in office, while he separated himself from the day-to-day running of the Trump empire (putting his sons Donald Jr. and Eric in charge), his fierce management style was carried over from his rough-and-tumble years in New York real estate. Trump values loyalty, relying on family members like daughter Ivanka and son-in-law Jared Kushner, who are both White House advisers. But aside from a few close aides and friends, Trump remains firmly at the center of his universe and relies heavily on his own confidence as a seasoned face-to-face negotiator.

And Trump continues to reinvent the presidency in his own inimitable style. With immigration the centerpiece of his campaign, he began a crusade to build stronger borders almost immediately. He started with a proposal to ban people from seven majority-Muslim countries from entering the U.S.

KEY ACHIEVEMENTS

• Installed two Supreme Court justices and 187 judges to the federal bench for lifetime appointments.

• Signed the Tax Cuts and Jobs Act that made the most sweeping changes to the tax code in three decades.

• Defeated ISIS' caliphate and killed Abu Bakr al-Baghdadi.

DID YOU KNOW?

Trump was part owner of three major beauty pageants at the same time: Miss Universe, Miss USA and Miss Teen USA.

A huge fan of social media, Trump has sent as many as 142 tweets on a single day.

IN THEIR OWN WORDS

IT'S NOT JUST THE MODERN AGE: PRESIDENTS HAVE LONG INFLUENCED THE ENGLISH LANGUAGE

At 12:06 a.m. on May 31, 2019, President Trump tweeted out a confusing and perhaps partial message: "Despite the negative press covfefe"—gifting the country with a brand-new word. It turns out it was a misspelling of "coverage."

Trump's error has yet to make it into Merriam-Webster, but presidents have been credited with making up words that have become part of our lexicon, including these.

"PEDICURE" President Thomas Jefferson was known to use French words and phrases from his time living in Paris—such as pedicure, to refer to the care of feet, toes and toenails. He is also credited with coining more than 100 other words, including belittle and mammoth.

"SQUATTERS" President James Madison used the term in a letter to George Washington about the just-drafted U.S. Constitution, referring to a group of people in Maine who were occupying land that didn't belong to them.

"SUGARCOATED" President Abraham Lincoln coined this term in reference to secessionists who had tried to argue that their actions were constitutional, and he had to defend the use of the term when the government printer balked at printing it.

"MUCKRAKER" President Theodore Roosevelt accused journalists of "digging in the muck" in a speech, adapting the term "muckrake" to refer to what he perceived as unscrupulous reporters—though the term became used also to describe ambitious reporters.

"FOUNDING FATHERS" The gents credited with forming this nation may have come about in the 1700s, but it wasn't until President Warren G. Harding (a senator at the time) said it in a speech to the Republican National Convention in 1916, and used it again in 1921 in his inauguration address.

"IFFY" President Franklin D. Roosevelt made up this word to describe elements of Supreme Court decisions that he disagreed with, and helped popularize the term by responding to reporters' queries by saying, "That's an iffy question."

"FINALIZE" President Dwight D. Eisenhower is said to have adopted this term from a 1920s Australian book, though others credit President John F. Kennedy with popularizing the term when responding to a 1961 query about an upcoming trip abroad by saying, "We have not finalized any plans."

"MULLIGAN" An extra stroke awarded after a bad shot in golf, this is another Eisenhower term that made it into the mainstream. The 34th president was an avid golfer and is said to have used this word during a round of golf covered by the media in 1947.

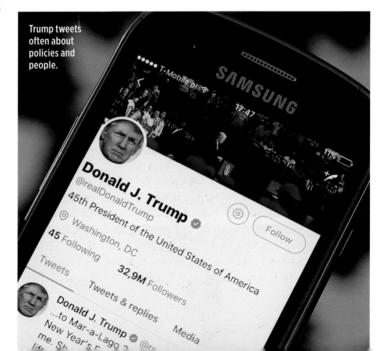

Trump tweets often about policies and people.

One of Trump's first cars was a 1956 Rolls-Royce Silver Cloud.

On June 16, 2015, Trump rode an escalator down to a press conference in NYC to announce his candidacy.

After two versions of the order were reversed in federal court, the Supreme Court upheld the third version, officially known as Presidential Proclamation 9645, which restricts entry into the U.S. for people from eight countries: Chad, North Korea, Venezuela, Iran, Libya, Syria, Yemen and Somalia. At the same time, he signed an executive order that significantly increased the number of immigrants considered a priority for deportation and reduced the number of refugee admissions to the lowest level since the resettlement program began. In September 2017, Trump announced he was canceling Deferred Action for Childhood Arrivals (DACA), Obama's program that allowed an estimated 800,000 young adults who were illegally brought into the country, called Dreamers, to work legally as adults. "I have a love for these people," insisted Trump, "and hopefully now Congress will be able to help them and do it properly." Amid protests from Democrats, Trump didn't back down, but the cancellation was put on hold by a court order. The Supreme Court is expected to make a final ruling sometime in 2020.

Trump's immigration policy hit a low note in February 2018 when he imposed "zero tolerance" for anyone caught illegally crossing the border.

Officials began the practice of separating minors from their families, sending children to government shelters and adults to federal jail as they awaited prosecution. What resulted was a publicity nightmare, as 2,300 children were depicted living "in cages," fueling widespread condemnation. Protests popped up in 600 cities across all 50 states, demanding that separated families be reunited. The American Academy of Pediatrics denounced the policy, claiming it would cause "irreparable harm" to migrant children. What the administration hoped would be a deterrent ultimately caused more harm than good. That June, Trump ordered that unauthorized families caught at the border no longer be separated, and those who had been could be reunited.

Despite setbacks, Trump continues to push through a plan to build a wall along the U.S.-Mexico border, although Democrats (who won back the House of Representatives in 2018) have repeatedly thwarted his efforts. By September 2019 though, the Supreme Court approved the reallocation of $6 billion to fund the wall's construction. And as of February 2020, 110 miles of the wall were completed, with 450 miles expected by the end of 2020.

He formed a relationship with North Korean leader Kim Jong-un.

"WHEN AMERICA IS UNITED, AMERICA IS TOTALLY UNSTOPPABLE."

DONALD TRUMP

During the campaign, Trump had vowed that his Supreme Court picks "will be great intellects, talented men at what they do—and women—but also be pro-life." And Trump has not disappointed his conservative fans. Justices Neil Gorsuch and Brett Kavanaugh have already been the decisive votes in cases related to immigrant detention, the death penalty and gerrymandering.

When he was elected, Trump also promised to replace NAFTA (the North American Free Trade Agreement, between the U.S., Canada and Mexico) and he met with Canadian Prime Minister Justin Trudeau to discuss new possibilities. The ball got rolling, and by November 2018, he proudly announced the revised agreement with a slightly different name, USMCA (United States–Mexico–Canada Agreement), which benefits all three countries. Describing it as a "historic transaction," Trump bragged, "I think my biggest concession would be making the deal."

To help businesses, the president repealed environmental regulations, then signed the Tax Cuts and Jobs Act, awarding an astounding $5.5 trillion in cuts for corporations and individuals. According to whitehouse.gov, the federal income tax owed by a household earning $75,000 fell from $3,983 to $1,739, a reduction of $2,244.

Until the coronavirus pandemic erupted in early 2020, unemployment had continued to fall under Trump, reaching a 50-year low of 3.6 percent in September 2019. But by May 2020 the virus had devastated the gains when 36.5 million people (and counting) filed for unemployment when businesses were forced to close, and people across the U.S. were asked to stay at home to combat the spreading disease. At press time, it remained to be seen if and when the economy would rebound.

As far as his foreign policy positions, Trump took aggressive action to confront Iran, including imposing sanctions on dozens of Iran-linked entities and refusing to recertify the Iran deal, according to whitehouse.gov. He has demanded that our allies share the cost of being the world's policeman, and under American pressure, most of our NATO allies have increased their defense spending.

Trump met three times with North Korean leader Kim Jong-un (in June 2019, he became the first sitting U.S. president to cross the 1953 armistice line separating North and South Korea). "At some point during the negotiation, things can happen," Trump said. After their historic summits, Kim committed to ceasing provocations and expressed a willingness to denuclearize, according to whitehouse.gov.

"Build the Wall" between Mexico and the U.S. has been a rallying cry for Republicans.

GOOD NEWS FOR TRUMP

Surrounded by supporters and his family, the president celebrated his impeachment acquittal in the White House on February 6, 2020.

In December 2018, he declared, "We have won against ISIS." Less than a year later, Trump celebrated another key victory in the war on terror when a special operations mission in Syria successfully resulted in the death of ISIS leader Abu Bakr al-Baghdadi in October 2019.

Still, controversy has plagued the Trump administration. The years-long investigation into Russian interference in the 2016 election led by special council Robert Mueller, which also looked into questions about links or coordination between the Trump campaign and Russia, resulted in no charges being brought against Trump himself and the president declared he was vindicated. But then in December 2019 the House of Representatives voted to impeach Trump for abuse of power and obstruction of justice. Still, the Senate acquitted him.

As he looks to secure a second term, he hopes to appeal to voters based on an increase in manufacturing jobs, a reduction in illegal immigration, increased funding for the armed forces, an overhaul of the health care system (including cutting drug prices), reforming Medicaid

and negotiating new trade deals. While his popularity among his loyal fan base has shown no signs of slowing down, it remains to be seen how voters in 2020 will react to his handling of the coronavirus pandemic.

2017–PRESENT

BORN JUNE 14, 1946, QUEENS, NEW YORK
EDUCATION WHARTON SCHOOL OF THE UNIVERSITY OF PENNSYLVANIA
POLITICAL PARTY REPUBLICAN
AGE AT INAUGURATION 70
VICE PRESIDENT MIKE PENCE
OPPONENT HILLARY CLINTON
OCCUPATIONS BEFORE PRESIDENCY REAL ESTATE DEVELOPER, TELEVISION PERSONALITY
OTHER OFFICES NONE
FIRST LADY MELANIA KNAVS TRUMP
NICKNAME THE DONALD

THE WILD WORLD OF
IMPEACHMENTS

NO PRESIDENT HAS EVER BEEN CONVICTED AND REMOVED FROM OFFICE. BUT THE PROCEEDINGS HAVE BEEN FASCINATING

★ ★ ★

The Clinton impeachment hearings were filled with salacious content.

THE WORD IMPEACHMENT HAS COME TO BE ASSOCIATED in this country mostly with two presidents: Andrew Johnson and Bill Clinton. More recently, a third (Donald Trump) joined their ranks. But all three were acquitted for their crimes by the Senate. Despite being the most infamous presidents connected to impeachment proceedings, they're not the only ones.

John Tyler

Whig John Tyler was the first president to face impeachment. Frustrated by Tyler's vetoes of popular Whig policies, Virginian Rep. John Minor Botts filed the first formal action in the history of the House of Representatives to impeach a president "on the grounds of his ignorance of the interest and true policy of this Government..." on July 22, 1842. The resolution was soon tabled for further consideration. A short time later, former president and Rep. John Quincy Adams approved a resolution in August 1842 condemning Tyler's misuse of veto power, but it went nowhere. And by the time Botts' resolution finally came to the House floor the following January, it was rejected by a vote of 127-83.

Andrew Johnson

Eleven articles of impeachment were brought forth in 1868 against Andrew Johnson, mostly for violating the Tenure of Office Act. Congress had passed this act one year earlier, to prevent Johnson from removing members of his Cabinet. So what did Johnson do? He removed Congress' ally Edwin M. Stanton, then appointed Lorenzo Thomas as interim Secretary of War.

Johnson's impeachment was riveting. One thousand tickets for each day of the trial were made available for other politicians and the public. The House of Representatives impeached Johnson 126-47 on three of the 11 articles; the Senate found him guilty with a vote of 35-19 for "high crimes and misdemeanors." A clear majority voted against the president, but the tally fell just one vote short of the necessary two-thirds majority to convict.

Of the 19 senators who voted to acquit, seven were Republicans, including Iowa Senator James Grimes, stating, "I cannot agree to destroy the harmonious working of the Constitution for the sake of getting rid of an unacceptable President." Johnson was ultimately acquitted, and the very Tenure of Office Act that lead to his impeachment was repealed in 1887 as being unconstitutional and therefore null and void.

Ulysses S. Grant

In 1876, near the end of Grant's second term, Democratic congressmen looking to drum up support pursued impeachment proceedings against the Civil War general. While many in Grant's camp had been impeached themselves for various offenses, Grant himself had never committed any impeachable offense. These proceedings were shelved, as the November elections would confirm a new president.

Harry S. Truman

In 1951, President Truman fired Gen. Douglas MacArthur from the Army, a move that enraged the Republican Senate, who held extensive hearings on the matter. Despite this, the House of Representatives was held by Democrats and therefore, they sat on the resolutions of impeachment put forth by congressmen George Bender and Paul Schafer.

Harry Truman's unpopular firing of Gen. Douglas MacArthur had Republicans shouting for impeachment.

Andrew Johnson avoided removal from office by just a single vote.

Richard Nixon

Perhaps the most famous threat of impeachment surrounded Richard Nixon after his associates broke into the Democratic National Committee headquarters in the Watergate Office Building on June 17, 1972. Nixon tried distancing himself from his associates, portraying himself as an innocent bystander and claiming he first learned of the break-in from news reports, saying he was "appalled at this senseless, illegal action."

Nixon claimed he never profited from public service, saying "I've earned every cent. And in all of my years of public life, I have never obstructed justice." But Nixon became caught up in the Watergate crisis and would be impeached on three counts: abuse of power, contempt of Congress and obstruction of justice. It was the cover-up—attempting to hide the tapes and cover the tracks of the conspirators—that created the greatest controversy. But Congress would never see the impeachment hearings through. Realizing he was not above the law, Nixon resigned in August 1974, the only U.S. president to do so.

Ronald Reagan

On March 6, 1987, Rep. Henry González put forth articles of impeachment against Reagan for his involvement with the Iran-Contra Affair. Four years later, González introduced articles of impeachment against Reagan's successor, George H.W. Bush, for starting the Gulf War. Neither attempt went further.

Bill Clinton

In 1998, Bill Clinton was the second president to be impeached, this time for perjury and obstruction of justice. His troubles actually began in 1994, when Paula Jones filed a lawsuit accusing Clinton of sexual harassment during his time as Arkansas governor. Clinton tried to postpone the lawsuit until after his candidacy, but three years after it was initially filed, Linda Tripp delivered recordings of her friend, former White House intern Monica Lewinsky, discussing her sexual relations with President Clinton to Paula Jones' defense council. Lewinsky claimed, "This was a mutual relationship, mutual on all levels, right from the way it started and all the way through. I don't accept that he

Richard Nixon remains the only president to voluntarily step down from office.

John Tyler was the first president to be threatened with impeachment.

had to completely desecrate my character." It was Clinton's comment—"I did not have sexual relations with that woman, Miss Lewinsky. I never told anybody to lie, not a single time, ever. These allegations are false"—that would spell disaster, as it came out that he had, in fact, had several physical encounters with her in the Oval Office.

Iowa Republican Sen. Charles E. Grassley commented, "The true tragedy in this case is the collapse of the president's moral authority. He undermined himself when he wagged his finger and lied to our people on national television, denying that relationship with Ms. Lewinsky. That did more damage to his credibility than any other single act.... The American people have a right to expect their president to be completely truthful, as they can expect you and me to be completely truthful."

By lying under oath, Clinton was found to be worthy of impeachment, with a 228-206 vote on the grounds of perjury and 221-212 on the grounds of obstruction of justice. But, like Johnson, the Senate was unable to convict Clinton, voting 55-45 against removing him from office.

Barack Obama

In March 2012, North Carolina's Rep. Walter Jones called on Congress, claiming Obama's approval of the CIA's use of drones in Afghanistan and Pakistan was impeachable. This failed, as did a 2013 hearing that accused the president of an abuse of power.

Donald Trump

After a whistleblower alerted the public to a July 25, 2019, phone call Donald Trump made to the Ukrainian President Volodymyr Zelenskyy—in which he allegedly threatened to withhold military aid to Ukraine unless Zelenskyy investigated presidential candidate and former Vice President Joe Biden—the word "impeach" began circulating through the Beltway.

Two articles of impeachment against Donald Trump were drawn up. During the proceedings, State Department official David Holmes, who testified he overheard a phone conversation between

Donald Trump declared victory after being found not guilty of impeachable offenses.

Trump and European Union Ambassador Gordon Sondland, said, "I then heard President Trump ask, quote, 'So he's going to do the investigation?' unquote. Ambassador Sondland replied that, 'He's going to do it,' adding that President Zelenskyy will, quote, 'Do anything you ask him to.'"

While many have drawn parallels between these proceedings and Nixon's, it seemed that Trump, who called the process a "disgrace", a "witch hunt" and a "hoax", as well as a majority of Republicans, shared the same sentiment as then House Minority Leader Gerald R. Ford had for the grounds of impeachment: "An impeachable offense is whatever a majority of the House of Representatives considers it to be at a given moment in history."

Donald Trump was impeached by the House of Representatives, but the Senate acquitted him along party lines on the two articles of impeachment (abusing his power and obstructing the congressional investigation). Senators found Trump not guilty of the first article of impeachment, abuse of power, by a 52-48 tally, and not guilty of the second article, obstruction of Congress, by a 53-47 tally.

SIMPLY THE BEST *and Worst* PRESIDENTS

ABRAHAM LINCOLN IS OUR GREATEST PRESIDENT, JAMES BUCHANAN IS THE WORST AND DONALD TRUMP'S PLACEMENT IS YET TO BE DETERMINED

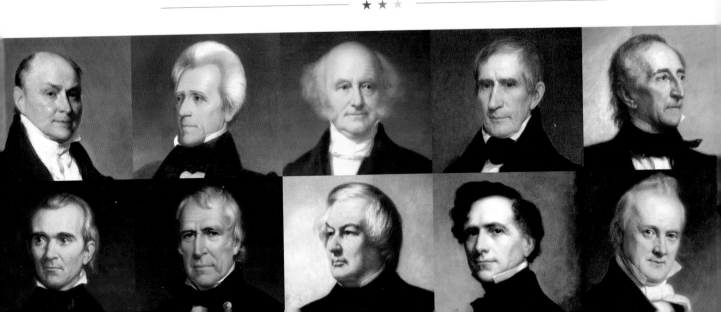

PRESIDENTIAL
RANKINGS

LEADERSHIP, MORALITY, CREATIVITY, BOLDNESS AND A RESPECT FOR ALL PEOPLE HELP CEMENT A PRESIDENT'S LEGACY

★ ★ ★

AT A TIME WHEN GROUPS AT BOTH ENDS OF THE POLITICAL spectrum consider the mere willingness to engage in interparty discourse to be inexcusable, the notion of "best" and "worst" presidents can be an explosive one. While political polarization is nothing new, the fuel for the modern fire certainly is. Social media platforms allow vague sources— some proven to be foreign governments—to spread misinformation designed to divide our nation and sway elections. Forceful partisan news outlets incite immediate emotional judgment of candidates, rather than encourage objective analysis of how their policies realistically affect all citizenry.

That's ironic, seeing that until 1987, the Federal Communication Commission's Fairness Doctrine required national broadcast networks to "cover controversial issues of public importance in an honest, equitable and balanced manner."

What most Americans can agree upon are certain virtues that inarguably successful presidents have shared. Foremost presidential historian Arthur M. Schlesinger Jr. identifies nine presidents— Washington, Jefferson, Jackson, Polk, Lincoln, Theodore Roosevelt, Wilson, Franklin Roosevelt and Truman—whom he calls "the immortals"—formative politicians with character traits our flag has come to represent. Schlesinger notes that foremost, all took "great risks in pursuit of their ideals, displayed boldness and creativity in office, and developed a deep connection with the needs, anxieties and dreams of the people," and "always displayed genuine intellectual curiosity that led them to listen as well as talk."

Schlesinger's immortals also forced the nation "to recognize incipient problems through sheer power of personality"—Jackson's charisma aroused a common understanding, even among less financially

The jury is still out on where Trump will rank.

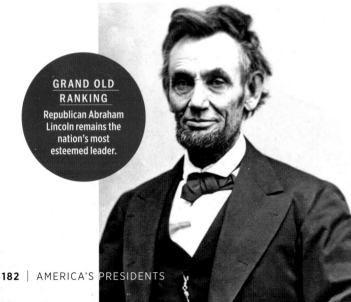

GRAND OLD RANKING
Republican Abraham Lincoln remains the nation's most esteemed leader.

HOW THEY COMPARE

WE TOOK FIVE PROMINENT POLLS TO DETERMINE WHO IS THE UNITED STATES OF AMERICA'S GREATEST COMMANDER IN CHIEF. AS PAST PRESIDENTS HAVE BEEN OUT OF OFFICE LONGER, THEIR LEGACIES HAVE HAD MORE TIME TO RESONATE WITH HISTORIANS, HELPING SUCH PRESIDENCIES AS BARACK OBAMA, WHO HAS MOVED UP CONSIDERABLY, AND HURTING ANDREW JACKSON, DROPPING HIM TO NO. 14. THOSE AT THE TOP OF THE LIST HAVE PROVEN THEY CAN LEAD THROUGH TOUGH AND CRITICAL TIMES, ESPECIALLY IF A WAR WAS FOUGHT.

	2016 RANKING	APSA 2018 Poll	SIENA 2019	WIKI 2019	C-SPAN 2017	Schlesinger 1996	AVERAGE
1 ABRAHAM LINCOLN	1	1	3	1	1	1	1.4
2 GEORGE WASHINGTON	2	2	1	2	2	2	1.8
3 FRANKLIN D. ROOSEVELT	3	3	2	3	3	3	2.8
4 THOMAS JEFFERSON	5	5	5	5	7	4	3.25
5 THEODORE ROOSEVELT	4	4	4	4	4	6	4.4
6 HARRY S. TRUMAN	6	6	9	6	6	8	7
7 DWIGHT D. EISENHOWER	7	7	6	7	5	10	7
8 WOODROW WILSON	8	11	11	9	11	7	9.8
9 BARACK OBAMA	18	8	17	11	12	N/A	12
10 LYNDON B. JOHNSON	14	10	16	12	10	14	12.4
11 JOHN F. KENNEDY	10	16	10	16	8	12	12.4
12 RONALD REAGAN	13	9	13	8	9	25	12.8
13 JAMES MADISON	15	12	7	13	17	17	13.2
14 ANDREW JACKSON	9	15	19	10	18	5	13.4
15 JAMES MONROE	12	18	8	18	13	15	14.4
16 JOHN ADAMS	16	14	14	15	19	11	14.6
17 JAMES POLK	11	20	12	20	14	9	15
18 BILL CLINTON	17	13	15	14	15	20	15.4
19 WILLIAM McKINLEY	19	19	20	19	16	16	18
20 JOHN Q. ADAMS	22	14	18	22	21	18	18.6
21 GROVER CLEVELAND	20	24	23	23	23	13	21.2
22 MARTIN VAN BUREN	24	27	25	26	34	21	21.8
23 WILLIAM TAFT	23	22	22	21	24	22	22.2
24 GEORGE H.W. BUSH	21	30	21	17	20	24	22.4
25 GERALD FORD	25	25	27	24	25	28	25.8
26 JIMMY CARTER	31	26	26	25	26	27	26
27 ULYSSES S. GRANT	29	21	24	36	22	34	27.4
28 CALVIN COOLIDGE	26	28	31	27	27	30	28.6
29 RUTHERFORD B. HAYES	27	29	32	28	32	23	28.8
30 BENJAMIN HARRISON	30	32	35	31	30	19	29.4
31 CHESTER A. ARTHUR	28	31	34	30	35	26	31.2
32 GEORGE W. BUSH	33	30	33	29	33	N/A	31.25
33 RICHARD NIXON	34	33	29	32	28	36	31.6
34 ZACHARY TAYLOR	32	35	30	34	31	29	31.8
35 HERBERT HOOVER	35	36	36	35	36	35	35.6
36 JOHN TYLER	36	37	37	37	39	32	36.4
37 MILLARD FILLMORE	37	38	38	38	37	31	36.4
38 FRANKLIN PIERCE	38	41	40	41	41	33	39.2
39 WARREN HARDING	40	39	41	39	40	39	39.6
40 ANDREW JOHNSON	39	40	44	40	42	37	40.6
41 JAMES BUCHANAN	41	43	43	43	43	38	42
TBD DONALD TRUMP	TBD	44	42	44	TBD	TBD	TBD

*RANKINGS DO NOT INCLUDE WILLIAM HENRY HARRISON AND JAMES GARFIELD, WHOSE TERMS WERE CONSIDERED TOO SHORT FOR EVALUATION; GROVER CLEVELAND'S TWO NONCONSECUTIVE TERMS ARE GIVEN A COMBINED EVALUATION. DONALD TRUMP IS CONSIDERED TOO NEW TO RANK.

minded citizens, which led to the vindication of a national authority against the Second Bank of the United States. Theodore Roosevelt's passion for nature magnetized support for his efforts to prevent raids on America's natural resources, while his unflinching optimism fueled the formidable task of breaking oppressive corporate monopolies.

The immortals, Schlesinger adds, served as "leaders of thought at times when certain ideas in the life of the nation had to be clarified." Washington embodied the concept of federal union. He recognized the powers of shared effort ("Let us animate and encourage each other") and honesty ("Be truthful and just ourselves to exact it from others"). Lincoln personified freedom and equality, and spoke to the importance of fortitude ("I am a slow walker, but I never walk back") as well as empathy ("I don't like that man. I must get to know him better").

In the spirit of the latter, we present a poll that aims to promote understanding of others and stimulate respectful discourse amongst all people, in a truly American manner. Our presidential rankings incorporate evaluations from some of the most respected scholars, historians and political minds in the world, valuable sources of highly academic views on presidencies that aren't necessarily represented in surveys open to the public. Note that this ranking leaves out Donald Trump's presidency; most surveys tend to wait until an administration is over before passing judgment.

All list positions are assembled from the averages of four prominent polls conducted over the past three years, as well as one conducted in 1996, the notable Arthur Schlesinger poll. Though the Schlesinger poll was taken before the offices of Presidents George W. Bush, Obama and Trump, and only includes Clinton's first term, its legendary participants make the poll a vital one. William Henry Harrison and James Garfield, both of whom died less than seven months into their first term, are not included in our rankings, as many poll participants feel such short careers do not provide proper grounds for making an informed judgment. Grover Cleveland, who served as both our 22nd and 24th president, is given one collective ranking. For scoring ties, the American Political Science Association (APSA) poll was used to determine ranking order.

Boise State University professor Justin S. Vaughn and University of Houston professor Brandon Rottinghaus assembled the 2018 Presidents & Executive Politics Presidential Greatness survey in conjunction with members of the Presidents & Executive Politics Section of APSA. Since the last APSA poll in 2014, Barack Obama rose 10 slots, and in his first evaluation, Donald Trump entered at last place, bumping James Buchanan up one spot. Of this poll's 170 respondents, 57 percent pronounced themselves Democrats, 13 percent identified as Republicans,

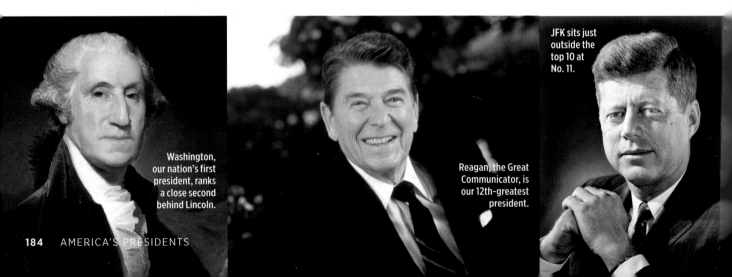

Washington, our nation's first president, ranks a close second behind Lincoln.

Reagan, the Great Communicator, is our 12th-greatest president.

JFK sits just outside the top 10 at No. 11.

27 percent self-reported as independents and 3 percent claimed other.

The 2019 Siena College Research Institute survey asks 157 historians, political scientists and presidential scholars to rank every president. Trump was ranked as the third-worst president in U.S. history, but because the Siena survey is conducted after each new president spends one year in office, Don Levy, the institute's director, notes that the sitting president often rises over the course of their term as "scholars begin to observe their accomplishments, assess their abilities and study their attributes."

To provide an interesting twist, we've also incorporated the current Wikipedia presidential master list, which compounds 20 separate polls conducted between 1948 and 2018 (including previous editions of other surveys we've included). Though Wikipedia is a community-controlled and monitored information source, all polls included are informed solely by historians and well-respected political minds, and all content on the presidential master list page is locked and cannot be altered by the digital public.

When you compare the 2020 rankings to a similar list we compiled in 2016, the biggest changes are Obama and Lyndon Johnson moving into the top 10, from 18 to 9 and 14 to 10, respectively. The rest of the top 10 was relatively unchanged; Andrew Jackson dropped out of the top 10, from 9 to 14; Polk, one of Schlesinger's "immortals," dropped from 11 to 17;

"THE BEST WAY TO PREDICT YOUR FUTURE IS TO CREATE IT."

ABRAHAM LINCOLN

Jimmy Carter moved up from 31 to 26. Also, not a single president received the same ranking from each poll. Even Abraham Lincoln, who's comparably ranked as our No. 1 president every time, is considered the third best by Siena.

The C-SPAN cable channel prides itself on being an impartial, balanced presentation; its poll aims to present nonpartisan results, and is informed by 91 university professors, academic authors and biographers, as well as decorated military personnel.

Perhaps the most revered poll in our list, historian Arthur Schlesinger's 1996 evaluation, was conducted before the true "digital age" began. Some claim its timing makes it more objective than others. Here, many of the century's most respected political scholars (some of whom are no longer living), rated presidents as great, near great, high average, average, below average and failure. Categories were assigned scores, results were calculated and presidents were ranked accordingly.

FDR's success during hard times over four terms lands him at No. 3.

Obama, ranked 18th in 2016, moved up to No. 9.

At No. 5, Teddy Roosevelt is a perennial top president.

Credits

COVER Clockwise from top right: Courtesy Everett Collection/Shutterstock; Glasshouse Images/Shutterstock; Courtesy Everett Collection/Shutterstock; Historica Graphica Collection/Heritage Images/Getty; GL Archive/Alamy; FineArt/Alamy; GraphicaArtis/Getty; Hi-Story/Alamy; Universal History Archive/Getty; VCG Wilson/Corbis/Getty; Alfred Eisenstaedt/Pix Inc./The LIFE Picture Collection/Getty; Bettmann/Getty; Bachrach/Getty; Burstein Collection/Corbis/VCG/Getty; Joe Sohm/Visions of America/Universal Images Group/Getty; Universal History Archive/Getty; History Archive/Universal Images Group/Getty; Niday Picture Library/Alamy; Pete Souza/Obama Transition Office/Getty; VCG Wilson/Corbis/Getty; Stock Montage/Getty; GraphicaArtis/Getty; Everett Collection/Shutterstock; Stock Montage/Getty; Time Life Pictures/Pix Inc./The LIFE Picture Collection/Getty; Harry Langdon/Getty; Bettmann/Getty; PhotoQuest/Getty **FRONT FLAP:** Brooks Kraft LLC/Corbis/Getty **1** White House Historical Association **2-3** YinYang/Getty **4-5** From left: YinYang/Getty; Muni Yogeshwaran/Getty; Ian Dagnall Computing/Alamy; Historica Graphica Collection/Heritage Images/Getty **6-7** Muni Yogeshwaran/Getty **8-9** Glasshouse Images/Shutterstock **10-11** From left: Ann Ronan Pictures/Print Collector/Getty; Pictures Now/Alamy **12-13** Francis G. Mayer/Corbis/VCG/Getty **14-15** Universal History Archive/UIG/Shutterstock **16-17** From left: Universal History Archive/UIG/Shutterstock; Stock Montage/Getty **18-19** Courtesy Everett Collection/Shutterstock **20-21** Universal History Archive/Getty **22-23** Burstein Collection/Corbis/VCG/Getty **24-25** From left: North Wind Picture Archives/Alamy; Science History Images/Alamy **26-27** From left: Pictorial Press Ltd/Alamy; Courtesy Everett Collection/Shutterstock **28-29** Bettmann/Getty **30-31** From left: The Art Archive/Shutterstock; Stock Montage/Getty **32-33** Niday Picture Library/Alamy **34-35** Painting/Alamy **36-37** DeAgostini/Getty **38-39** From left: Library of Congress; AP/Shutterstock **40-41** Clockwise from bottom left: Stock Montage/Getty; Print Collector/Getty; North Wind Picture Archives/Alamy **42-43** Ian Dagnall/Alamy **44-45** From left: Universal History Archive/UIG/Shutterstock; Courtesy Everett Collection/Shutterstock **46-47** Niday Picture Library/Alamy **48-49** Painting/Alamy **50-51** GL Archive/Alamy **52-53** Ian Dagnall/Alamy **54-55** Ian Dagnall Computing/Alamy **56-57** Ian Dagnall Computing/Alamy **58-59** GL Archive/Alamy **60-61** FineArt/Alamy **62-63** From left: Ian Dagnall Computing/Alamy; James K.W. Atherton/The Washington Post/Getty **64-65** Clockwise from top left: Bettmann/Getty; Underwood Archives/Getty; World History Archive/Alamy; Bettmann/Getty **66-67** RGB Ventures/SuperStock/Alamy **68-69** From left: Glasshouse Images/Shutterstock; Joe Sohm/Visions of America/Universal Images Group/Getty **70-71** From left: Courtesy National Archives Catalog; Corbis/Getty **72-73** Hi-Story/Alamy **74-75** History and Art Collection/Alamy **76-77** Clockwise from left: Courtesy Everett Collection/Shutterstock (2); Library of Congress/Corbis/VCG/Getty **78-79** VCG Wilson/Corbis/Getty **80-81** Everett Collection Historical/Alamy **82-83** Pictures Now/Alamy **84-85** PhotoQuest/Getty **86-87** The Artchives/Alamy **88-89** World History Archive/Alamy **90-91** History Archive/Universal Images Group/Getty **92-93** From left: Stock Montage/Getty; Library of Congress/Corbis/VCG/Getty **94-95** GL Archive/Alamy **96-97** Glasshouse Images/Shutterstock **98-99** From left: Hulton-Deutsch Collection/Corbis/Getty; Bettmann/Getty (2) **100-101** Pictorial Press Ltd/Alamy **102-103** Archive Pics/Alamy **104-105** Pictorial Press Ltd/Alamy **106-107** From left: Underwood Archives/Getty; Universal Images Group/Getty **108-109** From left: Courtesy Everett Collection/Shutterstock; Corbis/Getty; Shutterstock **110-111** PhotoQuest/Getty **112-113** From left: Hulton Archive/Getty; Library of Congress/Corbis/VCG/Getty **114-115** Clockwise from left: Allan Grant/The Life Picture Collection/Getty; Bettmann/Getty; US Navy/The Life Picture Collection/Getty; Underwood Archives/Getty; Wall/MPI/Getty **116-117** Bettmann/Getty **118-119** Clockwise from left: Palumbo/Library of Congress/Corbis/VCG/Getty; Keystone/Getty; Nat Farbman/The Life Images Collection/Getty; Thomas D. Mcavoy/The Life Picture Collection/Getty; Nara Archives/Shutterstock **120-121** Pictorial Press Ltd/Alamy **122-123** Clockwise from top left: Bettmann/Getty; Walter Kelleher/NY Daily News Archive/Getty; NASA Photo/Alamy; Bettmann/Getty **124-125** Alfred Eisenstaedt/Pix Inc./The Life Picture Collection/Getty **126-127** Clockwise from bottom left: Wenn Rights Ltd/Alamy; US Coast Guard Photo/Alamy; Karol Ciesluk/Shutterstock; Bettmann/Getty **128-129** Clockwise from top left: MediaPunch Inc/Alamy; NASA/Shutterstock; Stringer/AFP/Getty; Larry Burrows/The Life Picture Collection/Getty **130-131** Bettmann/Getty **132-133** Clockwise from top left: Universal History Archive/Getty; Bettmann/Getty; Corbis/Getty; AP/Shutterstock **134-135** Bachrach/Getty **136-137** From left: Everett Collection/Shutterstock; CPA Media Pte Ltd/Alamy **138-139** PictorialPress Ltd/Alamy **140-141** Bettmann/Getty **142-143** Clockwise from top left: Arnie Sachs/CNP/Getty; Alain MINGAM/Gamma-Rapho/Getty; Bjoern Sigurdson/AFP/Getty; Corbis/Getty

144-145 Hum Historical/Alamy **146-147** From left: Dirck Halstead/Liaison/Getty; Everett Collection **148-149** Michael Rougier/The Life Images Collection/Getty; Snap/Shutterstock; Bettmann/Getty; Dirck Halstead/The Life Images Collection/Getty **150-151** Wikimedia Commons **152-153** Corbis/Getty **154-155** Bettmann/Getty **156-157** From left: Arnold Sachs/Getty; Reed Saxon/AP/Shutterstock **158-159** Clockwise from top left: Dirck Halstead/The Life Images Collection/Getty; Wally McNamee/Corbis/Getty; Gina Ferazzi/Los Angeles Times/Getty; Dirck Halstead/Getty **160-161** Universal History Archive/Getty **162-163** From top: Paul J. Richards/AFP/Getty; Win McNamee/Getty **164-165** Pete Souza/The White House/Getty **166-167** Clockwise from bottom left: Lloyd Bishop/NBCUniversal/Getty; Dana Edelson/NBCUniversal/Getty; Pete Souza/The White House/Tribune News Service/Getty **168-169** Clockwise from top left: Andrew Holbrooke/Corbis/Getty; Chip Somodevilla/Getty; Mladen Antonov/AFP/Getty; Chuck Kennedy/White House **170-171** Courtesy Everett Collection/Shutterstock **172-173** From left: Jaap Arriens/NurPhoto/Getty; Ted Thai/The Life Picture Collection/Getty; Christopher Gregory/Getty **174-175** From left: Brendan Smialowski/AFP/Getty; Guillermo Arias/Getty; Mark Wilson/Getty **176-177** Clockwise from left: Joyce Naltchayan/AFP/Getty; AP/Shutterstock; Time Life Pictures/Mansell/The Life Picture Collection/Getty **178-179** From left: Photo12/Universal Images Group/Getty; Universal History Archive/Getty; Tasos Katopodis/Getty **180-181** From left, Row 1: Francis G. Mayer/Corbis/VCG/Getty; Courtesy Everett Collection/Shutterstock; Burstein Collection/Corbis/VCG/Getty; Bettmann/Getty; Niday Picture Library/Alamy; RGB Ventures/SuperStock/Alamy; Hi-Story/Alamy; History and Art Collection/Alamy; VCG Wilson/Corbis/Getty; Everett Collection Historical/Alamy Row 2: Pictures Now/Alamy; PhotoQuest/Getty; The Artchives/Alamy; PhotoQuest/Getty; World History Archive/Alamy Row 3: History Archive/Universal Images Group/Getty; GL Archive/Alamy; Glasshouse Images/Shutterstock; Pictorial Press Ltd/Alamy; Archive Pics/Alamy Row 4: Pictorial Press Ltd/Alamy; PhotoQuest/Getty; Bettmann/Getty; Pictorial Press Ltd/Alamy; Alfred Eisenstaedt/Pix Inc./The LIFE Picture Collection/Getty Row 5: DeAgostini/Getty; Ian Dagnall/Alamy; Niday Picture Library/Alamy; Painting/Alamy; GL Archive/Alamy; Bettmann/Getty; Bachrach/Getty; Pictorial Press Ltd/Alamy; Bettmann/Getty; Hum Historical/Alamy Row 6: Ian G Dagnall/Alamy; Ian Dagnall Computing/Alamy (2); GL Archive/Alamy; FineArt/Alamy; Wikimedia Commons; Bettmann/Getty; Universal History Archive/Getty; Pete Souza/The White House/Getty; Courtesy Everett Collection/Shutterstock **182-183** From left: Corbis/Getty; Courtesy Everett Collection/Shutterstock **184-185** From left: Francis G. Mayer/Corbis/VCG/Getty; Diana Walker//The Life Images Collection/Getty; Everett Collection/Shutterstock; Bettmann/Getty; Emmanuel Dunand/AFP/Getty; Corbis/Getty **BACK FLAP:** Muni Yogeshwaran/Getty **BACK COVER:** Clockwise from top left: Bettmann/Getty; Pictorial Press Ltd/Alamy (2); Ian Dagnall/Alamy; Pictorial Press Ltd/Alamy; Painting/Alamy; Library of Congress/Corbis/VCG/Getty; Ian Dagnall Computing/Alamy; Bettmann/Getty; Ian Dagnall Computing/Alamy; GL Archive/Alamy; Ian G Dagnall/Alamy; Pictures Now/Alamy; Pictorial Press Ltd/Alamy; Archive Pics/Alamy; GL Archive/Alamy; Everett Collection Historical/Alamy

SPECIAL THANKS TO CONTRIBUTING WRITERS

DENIS AUSTIN, JENNIFER BUSSELL, THERESA GAMBACORTA, EMILY GATLIN, BOB GUCCIONE JR., MIKE HAMMER, LIZA LENTINI, CAREN LISSNER, JAY McCLURE, RICHARD MARTIN, CAMILLA PAUL, JONATHAN ROWE

CENTENNIAL BOOKS

An Imprint of
Centennial Media, LLC
40 Worth St., 10th Floor
New York, NY 10013, U.S.A.

CENTENNIAL BOOKS is a trademark of Centennial Media, LLC

All rights reserved. No part of this publication may be reproduced, stored
in a retrieval system, or transmitted in any form or by any means (including
electronic, mechanical, photocopying, recording, or otherwise) without
prior written permission from the publisher.

ISBN 978-1-951274-40-5
Distributed by
Simon & Schuster, Inc.
1230 Avenue of the Americas
New York, NY 10020, U.S.A.

For information about custom editions, special sales and premium and corporate purchases,
please contact Centennial Media at contact@centennialmedia.com.

Manufactured in Malaysia

© 2020 by Centennial Media, LLC

10 9 8 7 6 5 4 3 2 1

Publishers & Co-Founders Ben Harris, Sebastian Raatz
Editorial Director Annabel Vered
Creative Director Jessica Power
Executive Editor Janet Giovanelli
Deputy Editors Ron Kelly, Alyssa Shaffer
Design Director Ben Margherita
Art Directors Andrea Lukeman,
Natali Suasnavas, Joseph Ulatowski
Assistant Art Director Jaclyn Loney
Photo Editor Keri Pruett
Production Manager Paul Rodina
Production Assistant Alyssa Swiderski
Editorial Assistant Tiana Schippa
Sales & Marketing Jeremy Nurnberg